LIVING
JOYFULLY
WITH
CHILDREN

LIVING
JOYFULLY
WITH CHILDREN

WIN & BILL SWEET

AWAKENING

ACROPOLIS BOOKS, PUBLISHER
ATLANTA, GEORGIA

LIVING JOYFULLY WITH CHILDREN
© 1997 Win and Bill Sweet

Published by Acropolis Books,
under its Awakening imprint

Second Printing, February, 2002
Printed in the United States of America.

No part of this book may be used or reproduced in any manner whatsoever
without written permission except in the case of brief quotations embodied in
critical articles and reviews. For information contact:

Acropolis Books, Inc.
Atlanta, Georgia
800-773-9923

http://www.acropolisbooks.com

Cover design by
Studio 2 Graphic Arts, Ltd.
Denver, Colorado

LIBRARY OF CONGRESS CATALOGING-IN-PUBLICATION DATA

Sweet, Win,
    Living joyfully with children / Win and Bill Sweet
        p.   cm.
    ISBN 1-889051-17-9 (pbk. : alk. paper)
    1. Parenting.   2. Child rearing.   3. Parent and Child.   I. Sweet,
Bill,   II. Title.
 HQ755.8.S94 1997
 649'.1--dc21   97–23182
                                                        CIP

THIS BOOK IS PRINTED ON ACID FREE PAPER THAT MEETS STANDARD Z 39.48 OF
THE AMERICAN NATIONAL STANDARDS INSTITUTE

∞

CONTENTS

To our children

Jill and Jim

&

our grandchildren

Deanna and Ryan

1.

DEAR
READER

THE OTHER DAY a good friend was reading over the manuscript we were working on for this book, and she exclaimed, "I wish I'd had this book when my girls were little!"

We smiled and replied, "We do, too. We wish we'd had this book for *our* children." But that would have been impossible, for it was the adventure of raising them that wrote the book, and what an adventure it was!

For a long time now, many friends and acquaintances saying, "Let us in on the secret," have asked us to write a book about parenting. At last we have a manuscript—a book for parents, grandparents, and all caregivers of children.

This book is a compilation of essays, each addressing a different area in which we found opportunities to make better choices in parenting. The essays are all based on our own experiences as parents and grandparents and upon experiences of other parents who have attended our workshops and seminars. All the examples we have used are based on real events, but we have changed the names except those of our children and grandchildren.

As we reviewed these essays, we relived the incredible journey of our active parenting days. Living with our children was exhilarating and joyful because we had developed new views of who children are and what good parenting is—views that were different from what we had been finding in our culture.

Dear Reader

How did we develop these new views? It all started after our second child was born. Our family was now complete. We had a nice home and two sweet, healthy children, but we looked at each other and said, "We have everything, but somehow life still feels incomplete. What are the mysteries of life, anyway? What is missing?" Asking those questions made us uncomfortable, and that discomfort changed our lives. From that day, we set out on a quest to discover the deeper meaning of life for ourselves, personally, and for the family as a whole. We began rethinking all of the normally accepted beliefs we had taken for granted for so long. As we considered our children and their place in our lives, that pondering naturally translated to rethinking children, family, and parenting.

As new parents we looked around at what the culture had to offer about parenting, and we were not satisfied with what we found. We wanted more for our children, and we set about finding it. Discovering new principles and inspiration from many enlightened and forward-thinking authors and mentors spurred us on into uncharted territory. All of this changed our lives *and* our parenting.

We were leaving behind much of what we had accepted before, and we were crossing into new frontiers of parenting possibilities. We dared to be different, not for the sake of being different, but because the new enlightening ideas were working. We began to reach UP and live our family life on a new and joyful level!

Through those years of searching we discovered a new way of loving our children. This book is about that new way to love children. The process of our quest led us to a broader range of parenting choices than we had known before. At the same time, we discerned ways to make more enlightened choices which led us to new experiences, which, in turn, gave us new insights. This book offers you many of these insights that may inspire you on your own parenting journey.

Welcome to the adventure!

WIN AND BILL

2.

THE JOY
OF PARENTING

*Bill: It was as if we were in some new world. Win and I
stood looking down at this tiny sleeping baby in her bassinet.
Yesterday was the excitement of Win giving birth to our first child;
today we were home, a family of three. Win and I were suddenly
totally responsible as parents of little Jill. I felt awed and helpless
about relating to this little baby. Win, at least, could nurse her. We
both sensed that being parents was going to add a vast new dimension to our lives. We had walked through the looking glass and
were now in a strange wonderland.*

NEVER HAVING BEEN PARENTS BEFORE, each day was an unexpected
adventure. Gradually, Win and I became more comfortable with
our new roles and saw that parenting could be a joy. Jim was
born on Jill's third birthday, and we now had a lovely little family of
four. Although we were much more prepared for a baby this time, we
were finding that parenting two children makes a very busy life. In
addition to our attention to the children, Win and I began to give
attention to issues of the family as a whole and the environment
which we were creating for our family.

We learned that one of the greatest privileges of parenting is to
create a family environment in which children's lives are happy,

healthy, and fulfilled each day of childhood and on into adulthood. In such an environment, the children thrive, and their innate enthusiasm brings a magical touch to our lives. Our challenge as parents is to cherish the children's zest for life and incorporate it into a joyous atmosphere in the home.

DISCOVERING JOY

Perhaps the greatest discovery that Win and I made as we were actively parenting our two children was the effect of *consciously* choosing a theme for the home atmosphere. Every family home seems to have a dominant theme. Some common themes are *control, competition, fear, advancement, achievement,* or merely *survival.* These themes come from our cultural influence. If parents don't consciously choose a theme, one is usually absorbed from the culture without any conscious thought and affects all members of the family. Themes that are constantly present in our culture are continually being reinforced in the homes; therefore, these common themes become and remain dominant with little or no effort from the parents.

Before we were married, Win and I were each achievers to some degree, so we automatically adopted the achievement theme as we set up our home. Each day for us was an opportunity for achievement. It wasn't until our second child, Jim, arrived that we began to question many aspects of our lives that we had taken for granted. "Is our home environment really valuable for the family?" we pondered. Then we realized, "There is something missing. The way we are living now isn't quite right."

First Win and then I, too, became convinced that we could and should find a way to set a more uplifting atmosphere for our home. We knew we would have to devote time and effort to do this, but the extra nourishment could have a big payoff for the whole family.

The breakthrough for us came with the word *joy.* To us the word had always meant something much greater than happiness, but we hadn't analyzed the meaning of the word much further. We did notice that sometimes we experienced a sense of well-being and delight as we were parenting. This feeling was not caused by what anyone in the family was doing; it seemed to be an expressing of ourselves as a result of doing parenting—feeling very right about doing it, and being very enriched by the parenting experience. "What is this?" we asked. The only word we had to describe this was *joy* with a very special meaning—*joy* that flows *from* us, not something that comes *to* us from others. Based on that definition, we chose *joy* as the theme for our home. We learned that as we brought that theme to mind several times each day, we established an atmosphere and environment that subtly affected the children and our family life.

Our first attempts at living joyfully with our children were exciting. We found when we consciously invited that joy to flow from us in our interaction with Jill and Jim, we spoke with a lilt in our voices and felt lifted. These were moments of carefree enjoyment with our children in their world. There was a glow about Jill and Jim, and they were creative and relaxed in a new freedom. This was the natural way for them to be, and it was contagious. We found *ourselves* getting back to that natural state as well. The excitement came from seeing how successfully and immediately the atmosphere of joy nourished us and the children.

The prospect of continually living joyfully with our children was tantalizing. However, we had difficulty maintaining the atmosphere for long periods because we tended to let little worries and concerns creep in and dampen or eclipse the joy. "Will they hurt themselves?" "Will they damage something?" "Shouldn't we enforce a bedtime?" "Are they eating enough?" "Shouldn't they be wearing jackets?"

THE TRUE SELF

"How do we make joyful living a more consistent reality?" we wondered. Approaching this perplexing question brought to mind something that we'd discovered a few years before when we were searching to gain more insight into the meaning of life. We had encountered a new view of our identity which rang a bell for us: *true* Self—a Self that we cannot see in the mirror, our perfect reality and essence.

Applying this knowledge of a true Self as a family principle promised to be as important as the theme of *joy* in satisfying and ful-filling that which was missing in our lives. The principle of true Self and the theme of joy melded to reveal another discovery: *The only way we could continually live joyfully with the children was to change the way we saw the children.* By seeing them as little people with an unconditioned innate sense of their true Self, we could drop our fears for them, and instead, trust them, or more specifically, trust their sense of their true Self. Small children do not have the words or mental concepts to be consciously aware of their true Self, but we found the children did seem to have an intuitive sense that operated as a positive factor in their lives. Of course, we wisely guided them out of hazardous situations and placed wholesome food before them; but by seeing them in this new way, we no longer needed to fear for them. Then it became clear to us that *to live joyfully with children we had to live without fear for them.*

Trying to live without fear for our children was the most difficult change we had ever attempted. We were determined to be responsible parents, and from the culture we kept receiving all sorts of fearful suggestions under the guise that responsible parents *should* have these concerns and fears. The only way we could deal with these subtle fearful suggestions was to absolutely reject them with a determined, "Not in our house!"

Once, a sincere young man came to our door promoting some religious pamphlets. After a quick perusal, I could see that the messages in the pamphlets were based on the fear of death. I simply said, "There is no fear of death in this house." The astonished young man quickly left.

OUR FAMILY SECRET

As the children grew to the stage where they had their own friends and outside activities and began watching some television and movies, they, too, were exposed to suggestions to be fearful. This presented a new challenge to our living joyfully as a family. Win and I were finding it difficult as adults to keep our minds free of fears. How could our children keep themselves free of the fears being projected at them from outside the family and not bring those fears home?

We couldn't simply tell the children not to be fearful or not to accept fear. Fear and worry are so contagious that it would have taken far more will power to resist than is reasonable to expect from children. The prospect of losing the magic from our family atmosphere because of outside influences of fear made us search for a new approach. We wanted the children to function normally in their outside world, but we also wanted them to be free of the fearful suggestions from that world. Wouldn't the approach that had enabled us to drop our own fears for them—recognizing their true Selves—also apply to their interaction with the outside world? "Yes," we agreed. "Recognizing the true Self for themselves and others is what will enable them to stay free of fears."

We had enough experience with our own friends to know that the subject of true Self was not something the children could talk about with their friends. Just as we had learned to keep that subject to ourselves, the children would also have to keep it to themselves as they played with their friends.

The idea of a family secret was born. It wasn't a secret about our family. It was a secret about everybody, but one that most people were not ready to understand; therefore, we would talk about it within our family but not outside our family. We explained to the children that we would keep this secret to ourselves, not because we wanted to keep their friends from knowing it, but because it was not kind to their friends to talk about something they would probably not be ready to understand.

The power of this secret for the children was that they could now view their friends as nice people who had just lost touch with their sense of their true Self and were, therefore, susceptible to suggestions of fear from the culture. This view freed our children to quietly disregard the fears and fear-based actions of their friends, and in this freedom, to support the *joy* theme of our home.

> **Win:** *One vivid example of Jim's use of this secret occurred when he was about twelve. Some larger boys at school threatened to beat him up after school if he didn't bring them some money after lunch. During lunch, he was telling me about the situation, wondering what to do about this threat. He concluded, "Those boys are just afraid, that's why they're acting that way. I might get beaten up, but I'm not going to be afraid. I won't give them money and lose my freedom."*

When the boys confronted Jim in class after lunch, he looked at them firmly and said, "No way am I going to give you any money."

The boys stared at him in astonishment. Jim stared back. They walked away and avoided him after that. Jim was glad that he knew the family secret.

The joy of parenting is not something that just happens. For us it is a theme that we choose, support, and honor. Of course, the parenting years are filled with countless necessary activities—changing diapers, cooking meals, helping with homework, resolving conflicts. You ask, "Where's the joy? Where's the time for joy? What is the basis for it? What does it feel like?"

This joy is an indescribable quality that stems from an ongoing and underlying sense of rightness combined with a spirit of adventure. The rightness comes from knowing that it is right that the children are with you and that you are with the children. Each of you is in the right place at the right time. They are enriching your lives and you are enriching theirs. But this rightness alone is not enough; there must also be the spirit of adventure.

The adventure is one of moving out from the traditional attitudes, beliefs, and worries about children into new frontiers of honoring and trusting the children, caring for their home environment in a new way, and establishing freedom from inappropriate influences of the culture. The excitement each day of being in new territory with the children is the spark that transforms parenting into *living joyfully with children*.

3.

HONORING PLAY

LL SHE WANTS TO DO IS PLAY. I have to *make* her do something productive." Deep in the puritanical roots of our culture is the belief that play is frivolous, a waste of time, and even somewhat sinful. As children grow, parents seem to become less and less tolerant of play. Perhaps this is because they are beginning to judge the quality of their parenting by how much of their children's time is spent doing something productive. Many parents believe that to play is to be idle, and, therefore, is not constructive or worthwhile.

Academic achievements and competitive sporting accomplishments are often the bases for how we judge what is productive. It's an easy trap because academics and competitive sports can be easily measured, and parents tend to be very competitive with other parents through their children. "Tommy hit two home runs in last week's game." "Mary has been promoted to third grade; she's too smart to waste her time in second grade." Parents unknowingly use their children in this kind of competition in order to feel more worthwhile themselves. If Judy's son, Jeff, runs for the winning touchdown and has a 3.7 grade point average, she feels assured that she's a great mother. Jeff's accomplishments fulfill her own emotional needs.

These attitudes and standards miss an important purpose of parenting, which is to help children develop a solid, strong emotional core—that place from where automatic responses to life come—so they will grow confidently and joyfully and meet life with equanimity.

If parents have a problem with play, their child will miss out on one of the most important mechanisms for positive development.

During the children's middle childhood years and on into the teens, the term *play* is generally dropped altogether, along with the idea of play itself. Do you ever hear the mom of a sophomore in high school say, "Tom is taking the next hour off to play, to be free to do anything he desires"? Now, fast forward to the stress-related problems of adulthood which are so often caused or exacerbated by the lack of free time in an adult's life. *Consciously* scheduling play time, quiet time, or free time, that is not time watching television, is almost unknown in our culture—yet play is so important.

All people, especially children, have an innate urge to play. Scientists have studied playfulness in animals and have determined that playfulness is an essential quality of all advanced mammal species. Interestingly, the scientists have found a close correlation between playfulness and certain physical characteristics—the stronger these characteristics, such as the flatness of the face, the more playful the animal is genetically intended to be. And what about humans? You guessed it! Based on these physical characteristics, humans are genetically intended to be by far the most playful creatures of all. It is our nature to play!

PRESERVING CHILDHOOD

What is the purpose, or the point, of childhood? The purpose of the long human childhood is to prepare for the fruition in adulthood of a special potential made possible because of the length of childhood. To be fully effective toward this fruition, childhood must be supported and revered by communities and families as a cherished commodity. Childhood is precious.

Play, in and of itself, is one of the strongest and most valuable contributions to fulfilling the purpose of childhood, and therefore, also deserves to be honored. Play is a freedom for children that yields a healthy emotional core and joyful attitudes. The child who has enjoyed much free play during childhood moves smoothly into adulthood.

Our childhoods were quite different from today's normal childhood. We were allowed and encouraged to be much freer than children are these days. We had no homework until junior high school. We came home from school and played—whatever that meant to us that day. Our mothers didn't have an after-school schedule of events for us. Except for our chores, which were not excessive, we did as we wanted. There was no television, so we weren't tempted to sit around. We both initiated projects involving activities we loved to do. If we wanted to play with a friend, we arranged it. If we wanted to go to the library or to the park, we were free to go. "Just be home for dinner," was our only guideline.

Childhood, as intended by the human biological, intellectual, and emotional pattern, is designed to provide the opportunity of growth in a relaxed, free, and happy environment of play. This growth design accommodates the gradual maturing of humans toward an adulthood that is based on intrinsic physical and emotional strength, a freedom from fear, preservation of enthusiasm and creativity, and critical and creative thinking. Human intelligence unfolds beautifully through play.

Childhood as nature intended is, unfortunately, rapidly disappearing. The word *childhood* used to connote a time of play and freedom which might last at least until high school; now childhood ends for many children at five years when soccer practice begins.

Childhood ends so prematurely, in other cases, because of the explosion of fear in our culture over the last years. "Is it safe to let my kids walk to the park?" parents and other caregivers ask. "Something terrible might happen." Yes, we seem to be hearing about terrible events more and more now, but is increasing fear warranted? A recent study revealed that the crime rate has gone down, but the *reporting* of crimes to the general public has gone up significantly. The actual occurrences of violence and crime are no more frequent than they were many years ago, but television brings every sensational incident right into our living room making it seem as if danger lurks uncontrolled on every corner, every moment.

Of course, parents need to teach their children *wisdom*, but not to cower in *fear*. A recent phenomenon in our culture has developed as many parents are not allowing their children to be alone outside *at all*. This may guarantee that a child is physically safe, but what about a child feeling emotionally safe from the significant effect of fear itself? Many latchkey children are instructed not to leave the house or answer the telephone or the door. While this may seem wise in the present culture, there has to be a better way. Scared prisoners cannot live happily, healthily, or creatively.

A working mom decreed that her daughter must never be alone, but must *always* be with a friend or family member. When the mom quit work, she suddenly realized her daughter was terrified to be alone at all. "I didn't think it through when I told Patty she must never be alone," the mother admitted. "Now she won't even go out alone to get the mail at the street corner."

Another infringement on free play is taking place as parents are demanding that teachers give their children hours of homework. The motivation usually isn't academically oriented, but simply to keep little Joe or Jessica out of trouble after school. Children are to be busy, but not busy *playing*. If children are sitting quietly doing nothing, they are often immediately instructed to get busy to accomplish something worthwhile. When we visited one family, we heard the mother say to her daughter who was sitting nearby, "If you can't find anything to do, you can fold the laundry."

When we consider the value of joyful attitudes and a healthy emotional core, it becomes clear that play, idleness, or free time can be the most productive and valuable part of the day.

THE VALUE OF SOLITARY PLAY

Solitary play is important for children of all ages and adults as well. This is an avenue for a child (or adult) to do the most important bonding of life's experience—bonding with herSelf or himSelf. The stronger this bond, the more stable the emotional core, the clearer is consciousness, and the more joyous, fulfilled, and fruitful is the child's life.

For small children, solitary play furnishes a time to quietly enjoy getting used to *me*, as well as developing a comfortable bond with *me*. There is a direct relationship between the strength of this bonding with Self and emotional strength through life in general. We're pleased when our grandson, Ryan, puts on one of his audio tapes of delightful children's songs and sprawls on our big chair to listen. Many adults would call that behavior withdrawn and be alarmed. In our view, it is one of Ryan's lovely and valuable forms of solitary play.

Solitary play is the most freeing for young children—the little ones who recognize the presence of another child as a threat to their peace and their own decisions about how they want to play. In their view the other child is a *thing:* a disturbance, a bother, and a grabber of their toys. They may not be mature enough yet to even recognize that this other child is a *person.* They are just aware that their personal space has been invaded. Until a child is mature enough to be able to negotiate, compromise, and cooperate, *and still have fun,* solitary play is the most comfortable and enjoyable. Young children do, at times, successfully play together, however, we have seen many situations in which two or more children are together, supposedly playing together, but in reality the children are merely contending for toys and space. Instead of an interval of free play, this contentious interaction is a trying time for the children and often for the parents as well.

Many parents of small children go to great lengths to have their children play with other children. "Bobby just turned one. It's time for him to learn socialization skills." But look closely. What is Bobby really learning? He may well be learning to fear, to fight, and to defend. "What is this that is grabbing my new red dump truck?" Bobby experiences frustration, anger, and violation of his space and himself. This is not positive socialization, but quite the opposite. Little ones who are not forced to go through these kinds of experiences, which can fragment the emotional core, are much better prepared *when they are more mature* to positively begin to develop important socialization skills. They have not built up a pattern of frustration, fighting, and defense that must be overcome before the positive patterns can be learned. Some children never do overcome the negative patterns caused by prematurely imposed interaction and continue to have socialization problems as adults.

The longer small children are encouraged to play freely all the time, the better they will meet life in general, and the more quickly they will learn the academics at the appropriate time. The appropriate time is often much later than people think.

During the middle childhood years, children who have been allowed to establish a secure sense of Self through opportunities in the earlier years to comfortably bond with Self, can begin to experience genuine positive play with other children, and they will be able to enjoy being alone to play as well. It's never too late to begin giving children plenty of chances to play. If the parent does not adopt the principle, *play is valuable*, until a child is in the middle childhood years, it may be a little more difficult to encourage the child to enjoy play. Play is not generally considered valuable during the middle childhood years.

> **Win:** *Wendy wailed into the telephone, "I'm going crazy. Andrea has been out on the patio for forty minutes bouncing her basketball around. What a waste of time! I want to march out there and tell her to get busy doing something worthwhile, but for some reason, I hesitate to do it."*
>
> *"Your intuition must be telling you to leave her alone,"*
> *I responded. And leave her alone, Wendy did.*

Even though Wendy was tempted by cultural conditioning to take control of the way Andrea was spending her time that afternoon, she wisely didn't interrupt. Instead, she gave Andrea the opportunity to have private quiet time, without Mom's interference. Wendy may not have realized what a wonderful gift she gave her lovely young daughter that afternoon.

Adults tend to believe that children need to be busy with others or to be engaged in worthwhile measurable activities in order to be accomplishing something. But often a very important activity can appear to other people as though *nothing* is going on. A child may seem to be idle when, in fact, the child is accomplishing important nourishment of her or his emotional core, mind, and consciousness: sorting out skills, experiencing intellectual advancement, and strengthening creativity. No one can enter that invisible place and see exactly what is going on. We adults know it is very stressful to be on the go all of the time with pressure after pressure to move from activity to activity. We forget children need to have quiet spaces in their days—even more than adults do—in order to accommodate the function of childhood. Quiet spaces relieve the pressures that are so often completely mysterious to children. All they know is that they are supposed to be going to this lesson after doing that homework, and sometime squeezing in their chores.

For a child, the reality adjustment to the adult world is difficult at best and traumatic at worst. Play helps children to adjust to the adult world and to mature smoothly and creatively according to their own personal timeline. Andrea needed space just to collect herself in a mindless, fun activity away from the pressures of what must have been a very complicated world to her.

Andrea doesn't always play alone. She has many friends and plays with them often. During these times, especially if no adults are around, she has the opportunity to learn give and take, negotiation, compromise, cooperation, thoughtfulness, and consideration. These are all important socialization skills that are learned almost entirely within the family structure and during free play with other children.

DON'T PUSH ME

When the little ones are allowed to spend as much time as they wish in each phase of the growth cycle to just play and have fun, they are like new plants which, given just the right conditions of light and water and soil, grow deep roots in the ground. If children are constantly being pushed forward—out of diapers, away from the bottle, into preschool, then into school, and then into sports and music lessons—usually before they are ready for each step along the way, they rarely have time to establish their own strong root system. The beginning of each new developmental stage is much easier and more natural if solid roots have been formed in the previous developmental phase, rather than the child being pushed forward from roots weakened by Mom's and Dad's high expectations and intense pushing. Sometimes it isn't the parents who do the pushing. It can be the school system, other teachers, and extended family members, as well as peers and their pressures.

Our daughter, Jill, began taking organ lessons when she was seven and by the time she was twelve, she had blossomed into a confident organist. She seemed to have natural talent and enjoyed her music immensely. Her teacher, recognizing her talent, often suggested that we enter her in competitions. We asked Jill if she wanted to do so and she always declined, "It's too much work preparing for contests; it wouldn't be any fun. What's the point?" We agreed with her. We wanted her to *enjoy* music on her own terms.

As the lessons continued, her teacher pushed her so hard to advance that one day she exploded, "I get frustrated because he gives me so much work to do for each lesson that I never have time to play the pieces that I've already learned and would really enjoy playing." She ended with, "I'm tired of this. I'd like to quit lessons and just enjoy playing the music I have learned and want to play." We were happy to oblige, and called the teacher to tell him she was quitting. He was incredulous. He actually accused us of being irresponsible parents not to force her to continue, "because she has so much talent." He was, without realizing it or intending to do it, dishonoring her by pushing her toward his objective, not hers.

For awhile, Jill did play and enjoy the pieces she had learned, then her interest in the music tapered off. For two years, she seldom touched the organ. Then one day she announced, "I would like to take lessons again. This time I want to study classical music." We engaged a new teacher of classical music and Jill resumed, did well, and thoroughly enjoyed herself. The two-year hiatus had actually enhanced her joy of playing the organ. Her time at the organ was wonderful play time for her, and she still enjoys her music.

SPACE TO BE

The principle here is *space to be*. Everyone who works with plants knows it is important to start plants with plenty of room to grow; crowded plants do not thrive. Hot-house plants look great for awhile, then falter because they are intrinsically weak. As we learn to give our children the same *space to be* that we give our plants, we'll see the same good results. In our culture there is little encouragement to provide time and *space to be* for children, and especially little encouragement to provide time for children of the middle years and teens to play and be free. Giving children space requires thought, consideration, and planning.

Children need to be able to sort out *me* in relation to their own world and whatever comes into that world from other people, events, and feelings. Every intrusion into the *me* world is an adjustment and sometimes a trauma. Play is a haven, an insulator, a place for retreat in which to adjust, regroup, gain access to creativity, and learn skills, such as trial and error problem solving. In addition, free play is empowering for a child (and an adult).

Honoring Play

The kind of play that fulfills childhood will pass the following play test:

- *Is the activity free of competitive tension?*
- *Is it child-initiated, child-directed, and child-motivated?*
- *Is it really fun for the child, according to the child's criteria?*
- *Is it free of any preprogrammed academic or performance requirements?*
- *Is it always a winning experience?*
- *Can the child be spontaneous and free of adult judgments?*
- *Are the computer and television off?*
- *Is there opportunity at times for solitary play?*
- *Is it free of pressure and fear?*
- *Is there opportunity for fantasy, innovation, and make-believe?*

True free play would ideally include the criterion that there are no adults present. When children are playing, they often feel they are on stage performing if there are adults around—even if the adults aren't intently watching. Little children are not as self-conscious as older children who often have one eye on the adult to see if the adult thinks they are "playing right." Children often call out, "Watch me!" or "Look at how high I can jump!" This is not free play.

Contrary to popular belief, during free play children learn much of immense value that prepares them for all of life: negotiation, organization, problem solving, connectivity, relatedness, selectivity, adaptiveness, innovation, strategy, and responsibility. With these valuable attributes in place as a result of their own discovery through free play, children are well-prepared to learn academics very efficiently and well, and in a much shorter time than is currently the educational timetable for children. For their children of all ages parents would be wise to go out of their way to promote play and discourage unnecessary experiences of being *taught*.

A fine parenting principle is: *Let children learn by their own self-direction through play, and whenever possible, refrain from teaching them.* Of course, safety awareness needs to be taught, but in other areas, instead of imposing a program of teaching, provide children maximum opportunities for free, self-stimulated play that are not dependent on a deluge of toys, projects, or achievements to accomplish. In this freedom children will joyfully learn and create their own special kind of wealth.

A parent who honors a child's natural joy of play honors the child. An honored child feels valuable, and feeling valuable is the greatest longing of all human beings. There are three important ways to honor play for your children:

- *Encourage solitary play.*
- *Provide opportunities for authentic free play with other children.*
- *Play with your children on their terms.*

These people we call *children* are intended by the pattern of the universe to play, to have time to simply *be*, to grow at their own pace, to have fun, to be loved and cherished, and to be free to enjoy and use their gift of imagination. The essence of childhood is play.

4.

WHERE DO THOSE
IDEAS COME FROM?

K AREN, GET THESE NOISY KIDS OUT OF HERE!" Dad is watching
his Sunday afternoon game on the family room television
set. Tommy and Amy are providing dramatic sound effects
as they play with their fire engine and truck on the family room floor.
Mom dutifully stops what she is doing, herds the kids out the back
door, and then tries to resume where she had left off when the out-
burst from Dad erupted. But something troubles her. Where *do those*
ideas come from?

Where did her husband, Ted, get the ideas to call the children
noisy in their presence, eject the children from a part of their play
area without their understanding why, and expect *her* to solve *his*
problem? Ted is a normal, nice man and their marriage is o.k. Karen
muses that they didn't consciously agree to treat their children gruffly
or decide together that he should expect her to solve his problems.
So where *did* the ideas come from?

Karen asked Ted later, "Why did you say that in front of the kids?"

"Say what?" asked Ted.

"'Get these noisy kids out of here!'" Karen reminded him.

"Gosh, I don't know; it just came out. It was the fourth quarter,
the Colts were just about to kick a field goal. I'm sorry about that,
Honey, I just didn't think." Ted replied.

"I know you are, Ted. I just wonder why it keeps happening." con-
cluded Karen. Later she raised this question in one of our seminars.

Where Do Those Ideas Come From?

We, ourselves, had some experiences that led us to ask, "Where do these ideas come from?" What is the source of the ideas, thoughts, attitudes, actions, and reactions that are shaping and influencing so much of our daily lives? When we looked for answers, we found that the source of our own ideas was primarily *cultural*. It was the culture that gave us suggestions, habit patterns, belief systems, and ideas—all passed on to us through our relatives, peers, education, traditions, media, religions, politics, and even subliminally through the invisible consciousness of the culture itself. We saw that all of this influence is passed down from generation to generation, with each new generation adding its own new elements within the context of old ideas.

We began to picture ourselves as being at the front of a long line of generations extending from the mists of ancient history to the daylight of the present moment. Each generation overtly and subliminally passes along its cultural suggestions, ideas, patterns, and belief systems. Gradually some suggestions, such as younger daughters not being allowed to marry until the eldest has married, are traded in for new ones, such as daughters leaving home to have their own apartment and relating to men when, and as, they please. The elements of the culture include a lot of accumulated negative emotional baggage and old misperceptions that are not valuable to base our lives on today, like fear and guilt. There are valuable elements as well, like practicing good manners and being charitable.

A very large and complex collection of cultural elements affects all parts of our lives, including our attitudes about parenting. Ted acted out a familiar behavioral pattern, but not because he'd consciously chosen it as one might choose a particular brand of soup. He had unknowingly picked up a pattern of behavior, perhaps from his family or from the culture—television, friends, and role models.

When we began to realize we were not as in charge of our lives as we'd thought, we explored this subject at length. We wanted genuine *freedom to choose*; we did not want to be limited by the choices the culture presented. But before we could break free, we had to understand what was going on, so we consciously decided to learn about the culture and its effect on us.

We came to realize that the influence of the culture on our lives was much greater than simply the effect of our knowing the mores,

Where Do Those Ideas Come From?

traditions, and concepts of our parents and their parents and their parents before them. We could see that we were so accustomed to the presence of the past and present culture in our lives that we couldn't even recognize that it was affecting us. One day the idea suddenly came that the presence of the culture in our lives was, in effect, acting as an optical filter, obscuring or coloring what we perceived about our life experiences. We were wearing tinted glasses and didn't know it. These misperceptions caused by the cultural *filter* were really the root cause of most of the attitudes and actions which occasionally surprised us ("Why did I do that?") and which we often could not logically explain.

As we began to grasp the picture of the cultural filter line, we could finally begin to gain new perspective. We became aware that we were standing squarely at the front of the line, simply living and passing on belief systems of the culture. We were accepting and making the culture's ideas our own, no questions asked. Our ideas certainly were not ones we developed ourselves. It didn't take long to see that this was affecting our parenting.

Forms of the various belief systems change through the centuries and from person to person. But the

The Cultural Filter Line

cultural filter basics remain much the same—
fear, power, money. Parents continue wanting
the kids to do what they're supposed to do,
whatever is popular in that generation.
It's like an ever-deepening rut, and here
we are today at the front of a long line
of generations that, without thinking,
have been following along in that rut.

It was a big breakthrough in
our lives when we realized that in
order to be free of the negative
effects of the cultural filter,
we had to be willing to step

Stepping Out of Line

out of the line. In order to
step out of the line, we had to
understand the cultural filter
that is being passed down
through the generations. We
were beginning to do that.
Dare we step out of line? We've been
told since we were children not to
be out of line. Very simply, we found in
our own parenting experience and that
of others with whom we have worked,
that we must step out of the cultural filter
line enough to recognize it, to be discriminating, and say, "Ah, *that* is where
those ideas come from." In our new freedom we can adopt fresh new, enlightened ideas, principles, and attitudes
about children and our roles as
parents. Only then can we really *see* our
children as the individuals they are.

As we step out of the centuries-old line,
we may be out of line with much of the
culture, but we are setting ourselves free and
our children free.

5.

CRYING: WHEN IS IT O.K. AND WHEN IS IT NOT?

WHEN IS CRYING O.K., AND WHEN IS IT NOT? The answer is that crying is always o.k. for all age children, both boys and girls. Crying is an important emotional mechanism that serves many purposes. It is a way to relieve tension; reestablish equilibrium; and express fear, anger, frustration, disappointment, hunger, or discomfort. Crying may reveal pain or injury, and it is sometimes an expression of joy. Most people know this, yet many parents approach a crying child, even in the best case, with a comment like, "Don't cry, Honey." This is the wrong message to instill in a child's mind and consciousness.

Emotional problems experienced in childhood and in adulthood can be partially or even completely due to the edict early in life, "Don't cry." This edict easily and quickly translates in the child's mind as "Don't express your feelings; that is unacceptable." Even innocently saying, "Don't cry," meaning, "You needn't cry; Mommy will fix it," or "You're o.k.; don't be afraid," can be misinterpreted by the child and cause injury to the emotional core. Many adults spend much time and money with therapists trying to reverse the edict from their childhood, "Don't cry." The message they are trying to erase so they can freely express their feelings is: "Crying is unacceptable; submerge the feelings that cause you to cry."

Although children of both genders have heard, "Don't cry," these words are generally projected more at boys than at girls. One of the worst things to do to a boy is to say, "Boys don't cry." This is common in our culture and explains why boys have more problems with pent-up emotions than do girls. Their pent-up feelings can cause serious problems for others in their relationships as well. *Consciously* countering the cultural suggestion, "Boys don't cry," with assurances of the importance and value of crying when the impulse comes—including the teen years and beyond—can be one of the best actions parents can take to help prepare their boys for a brighter, freer future.

There are many consequences to giving a child the message, "It's unacceptable for you to cry." For small children, thumb sucking, attachment to a blanket or something soft, addiction to a pacifier, and perhaps later, addiction to cigarettes, eating disorders, and learning disorders are just a few that can, at least in part, be traced to this command. Children in the middle childhood years who are encouraged not to cry often become withdrawn, cease communicating with the family, and take on negative personality changes.

Adolescents suffer the same reactions as children in the middle years. Perhaps much of what the culture calls rebellious behavior can be attributed to adolescents having been conditioned not to cry. As with everyone, adolescents have to do *something* with the feelings that would be relieved by crying. When the harmless and natural avenue of crying is cut off, other ways of finding comfort or other consequences of discomfort materialize. Exhibiting reckless or belligerent behavior, driving too fast, drinking, smoking, using drugs, withdrawing, running up excessive credit card bills, and even contemplating suicide have all been outlets for pent-up frustrations for some adolescents.

The pattern of looking "out there" (for example, overeating), as compensation for the loss of something that is "in here" (permission to cry) is undesirable for people of any age, but especially undesirable for children. Children need to learn to appreciate the great value of themSelves. This appreciation forms the foundation for their own intrinsic strength and their ability to function successfully in relationships. If, instead of valuing themSelves, which would include experiencing the freedom to cry, they are forced to look elsewhere for a sense of value, their process of awakening to their own value can be seriously derailed or postponed. External activities that are often used to compensate for the loss of crying include overeating and anti-social behavior. The external compensations may seem to be minor factors in childhood, but they can become major problems if carried into adulthood.

Is there a principle here? Yes.
*Honoring a child's use of her or his own resources, in this case, crying,
to get through a difficult situation, honors the child and helps
the child honor herSelf or himSelf.*

Make it a strict policy never to say to your child, verbally or non-verbally, "Don't cry." This policy applies to babies as well as older children, because even though babies do not intellectually understand, they get the message in consciousness through the tone of voice and the atmosphere you carry.

Instead of "Don't cry," respond to crying without any anger or frustration and with comforting remarks of understanding. For example, "I know your scratched knee hurts. Let's fix it so it will feel better." Then calmly proceed to do that. "We know you want to go with Daddy, but this time you can't." Then guide the child to alternative attractions. "We understand how disappointed you are that your science project fell apart." Then give the child a big hug. "We're so sorry you didn't get asked to the prom; we know that feels awful." Accompany this with the most meaningful, loving gesture you can give to this child. These types of statements acknowledge and accept that crying is o.k.

Be prepared to let your child cry wherever you are. If you truly believe that crying is o.k. and should not be stifled, it won't bother you. If you are at home without guests, it is easy. If you are in a restaurant or at someone else's house, calmly walk out with the child and don't be embarrassed. Our concern must be for what is best for our children, not for what other people will think.

In all cases, at all ages, for girls *and* boys, the principle is:
Crying is o.k.

Crying: When Is It O.K. and When Is It Not?

There are five important supporting principles to that main one:

1 Try to correct or change whatever is *causing* the crying. Don't address the crying in itself.

2 When you have done everything that is reasonable and the crying continues, just quietly wait if you are sure you do not need medical assistance. Calmly, without experiencing any tension or fear, make the child and yourself as comfortable as possible. (You may want to use ear plugs.) Then soothe, comfort, and be patient. Remember, you have not failed because your child is crying.

3 When the crying is simply a manipulative trick, casually allow it, but ignore it. Children learn very quickly how to push the right buttons to get what they think they want. A parent who can't stand crying is at a definite disadvantage.

4 If a little fall would become a big tragedy by your reacting when the children start to cry, pretend you didn't see it or kindly make light of it so that they can make light of it as well. We've all seen children have a little fall or minor mishap and look at us to see if we're watching.

5 Refrain from using the moments of crying to try to talk the children out of feeling bad, to rationalize the sorrow away, to make corrections, or to give lectures. At that particular moment, a loving, quiet presence that includes recognition of the beautiful Self of your child is the best support you can give. Finding solutions, talking about principles, and planning how to go forward can come later.

Emotional stability is an important element in a positive life. One way it is measured is the degree of freedom an individual has from pent-up, submerged negative feelings. Crying is a wonderful and natural safety valve. A parent is wise, indeed, who never interferes with that safety mechanism. Don't say, "Don't cry."

6.

INTERACTION
VS. REACTION

D
ON'T pick up that awful, dirty thing!" screams Mother. Tommy
immediately becomes anxious and drops the fascinating,
muddy rock he has found and wants to explore. What does it
feel like? How does it look up close? How far can I throw it? Instead
of exploring, Tommy drops the rock and looks up at Mother with a
quivering lip and fear in his heart. "What is going to happen to me
now?" What could have been a marvelous opportunity for Tommy
to freely and eagerly interact with his world has just been aborted.
Instead of enjoying the moment, gaining confidence, becoming aware,
and developing various skills, he experiences disappointment and fear.

Children need to build a structure of skills in order to function
successfully in our unpredictable world. Accurate perception, critical
thinking, and decision-making are the types of skills that can develop
through experimenting and absorbing knowledge of the world in a
non-intellectual and indirect way. When children freely interact with
and explore their world—rocks, flowers, bugs, food, people, toys,
books, household items, clothes, knobs, and gadgets—they are learning through their natural curiosity.

Interacting freely means interacting without receiving commands,
directions, or input of any kind from adults. Even subtle innuendoes
can abort a child's adventure. Commands and directions are almost
always based on adult logic, the adult way of processing information,
and adult value systems, all of which are generally very difficult for

children to relate to without confusion and possibly fear. Tommy wasn't allowed to *interact* with his world; he had to *react* to his mother's anger.

Many parents believe that their task as a parent is to persistently direct their children from one task or activity to another. The children are pulled this way and that way according to the parents' own set of values and judgments, their personal agenda, and their program for the children. What of the children? Besides their time at home, they also have to contend with directions and instructions all during school hours. There is a numbing effect that takes place in consciousness when children have to continually react to commands or directions, especially when they have little or no understanding of purpose or reason. Sitting still for long periods is so counter to children's nature that the resulting stress is intense. Children are naturally guided to move about often and to function with short attention spans in order to fulfill the growth cycle gracefully. *Children need space in life to act freely.*

Since our children are not wandering around in a forest as wild animals do, it is not practical or feasible to eliminate all commands or limits, but in most households there are far too many of them. The few that are necessary, such as those pertaining to the child's safety, good health, and participating within the family structure can be communicated gently without causing the child trauma. There are times when we must ask our grandchildren to do something NOW, but those times are very seldom. If we must interrupt their free play, we allow plenty of transition time in order for the children to be able to move through the day smoothly and joyfully.

There can certainly be risk in allowing free interaction. In Tommy's case, it is the possibility of dirty clothes. Usually the risk is balanced by the desirability of the children having opportunities to develop skills and acquire knowledge. Doing this by their own process will serve children well in the future when the serious challenges arise and important decisions must be made. The children who have not personally acquired valuable experience and developed skills, strength, and ability to make their own productive judgments and decisions are at risk as they function in the world. Avoiding that risk is not difficult.

Interaction vs. Reaction

True *interaction* can only take place in an atmosphere of freedom and trust, whereas *reaction* generally takes place in an atmosphere of fear and confusion. Parents need to find a balance between *trusting* and *protecting* in such a way that they don't impose their fears onto the child. Children can become so weighed down by their parents' fears that they simply cannot function well in the world.

Ben spent his childhood as the only child of two loving, caring parents. His father was a reasonably successful business man, and his mother was an at-home mom. Both parents were artistic and cultured, and Ben grew up in a home that was frequently filled with classical music and refined conversation. One might expect that with this background Ben would have been well-prepared for his adult life. In fact, it has taken twenty years for him to get his life in order. What happened?

Ben's mother was raised in a religious background that was steeped in fear, and all through her parenting years she was very fearful as a person and a parent. She protected Ben to an extreme. Like Tommy's mother, if Ben's mother saw or imagined any risk to Ben as a result of his interactions with his world, she would fearfully step in, leaving him only the option of reacting to her fear. She ordered Ben to wash his hands frequently because of her fear of germs. When he became mature enough to travel by air, she would not permit it because of her own fear of flying. Through his childhood Ben gradually picked up her fears and developed additional fears about interacting with his world. As a young man, he found that he was nearly a hypochondriac about germs, his food, and his health. Further, he told us, "Whenever I travel in a plane, my stomach is tied up in knots and my fists are clenched."

Interestingly, Ben's father appeared easy-going as a person and a parent. Ben aspired to be easy-going too, but could only fake an outer appearance of confidence; inwardly he quivered under a heavy load of fears.

Ben carried the fears from childhood as pieces of unwelcome baggage. He could hardly make a decision because he feared it might prove to be the wrong one, and he kept sabotaging his adult life at crucial times. He was talented, outgoing, gregarious, and discriminating, so he usually had many fine friends. Ben found, however, that whenever he tried to form a deeper relationship with a woman, the risks of interacting so closely with her terrified him. He pulled back and effectively sabotaged his progress toward marriage. In effect, his mother's fears that stopped his childhood interactions had formed subtle fear patterns that were limiting Ben's life twenty years later.

This story has a happy ending. Ben worked hard in recent years to understand and appreciate his true value as a person. He didn't struggle to overcome the fears that he acquired during childhood, he merely realized that they never really belonged to him and that his true Self can't be hurt through close relationships. In fact, he has realized that his true Self can be expressed joyfully in marriage. Now Ben is finally free and his most recent relationship seems to be progressing smoothly toward marriage.

Parents who persistently impose directions, transfer fears, and unnecessarily assist or intervene prevent positive development for their children. Instead of giving the usual, never-ending deluge of commands to which children must react, wise parents converse with their children without value judgments, describe without editorializing, watch quietly, play with the children in their world, and praise generously. For example, Dad lies on the floor giving rapt attention to little Sarah, who is playing on the floor beside him. He doesn't try to interrupt her or excite her, he is just *with* her, entering her make-believe world and talking softly. Quiet, relaxed conversation in natural adult style, even if the child cannot understand everything, can be a lovely experience of intimacy for a child.

Tommy was deprived of the joy of exploration and discovery by his mother's angry command. Ben was deprived of personal freedom by his mother's fears. Most short-term parental objectives—like keeping clothes clean and excessively avoiding germs—are not important enough in the context of a child's whole life to warrant the price of that child losing the freedom to interact with her or his world.

Parents can accept the challenge to break the habit of issuing commands and dispensing fear, and instead, give children encouragement to interact with their world *on their own terms*. Supporting the fulfillment of children's natural curiosity and love of learning preserves patterns of interest and enthusiasm that will enrich their entire lives.

7.

An Invisible Resource

W HAT ARE YOUR OBJECTIVES AS A PARENT?"
When we ask that question in our seminars,
we get many answers:

- *Keep my children safe.*
- *Create family fun.*
- *Teach good citizenship.*
- *Provide a college education.*
- *Give them what I didn't, or did, have.*
- *Provide music lessons, dancing lessons.*
- *Help them reach their potential.*
- *Assure their participation in competitive sports.*
- *Teach honesty, integrity, and good manners.*
- *Keep them out of trouble.*
- *Be sure they keep up with other children.*
- *Keep them healthy.*
- *Make sure they behave properly.*

Of course, these are all legitimate answers to the question, but
there is another objective that, if fulfilled, makes all the rest of the
important objectives parents have much easier to achieve. This objective is the tender, loving care of the children's invisible resource,
which we call their *emotional core.* If your children's emotional core is

solid, strong, and intact, that splendid invisible resource will carry them from their early years through the rest of their lives in positive, joyful directions. With an emotional core in fine condition, children naturally soar into a life that is fulfilling. The bonus is that nourishing this resource in a child benefits not only the child, but the whole family.

Every human being has an emotional core. It is that place from which come the automatic reactions to life. The condition of the emotional core determines, for instance, whether or not an individual silently withdraws if relationships or circumstances become uncomfortable, throws a plate if a spouse says the wrong thing, gets sick if an exam comes back with a C grade, or sinks into depression if a schoolmate says something unkind. Pick any trying or difficult circumstance that average people may face in the course of a day, and some will fall to pieces emotionally or act foolishly, while others will face adversity calmly, wisely, and harmoniously. What causes the difference? The deciding factor is the condition of the emotional core, which affects every one of life's experiences. It is invisible, but it is constantly present in consciousness.

If the emotional core is in excellent condition, life's experiences will reflect that. If it is in poor condition, all of life's experiences can be a trial. Of course, there are many possible variations.

It is crucial to *consistently* care for the children's emotional core because they face challenges almost every hour of every day. Parents can't yell at a child, gruffly direct, roughly correct, and restrict freedom for six hours, then cuddle the child lovingly for a few minutes and have consistently cared for the emotional core.

If the emotional core has been consistently cared for up to the time the children pack up and walk out the door of their childhood home into the adult world, they will be well-prepared to handle college, employment, marriage, friendships, crises, big decisions, and other areas of life with confidence, efficiency, equanimity, wisdom, and joy. Important characteristics, attributes, and attitudes will function *automatically* when the emotional core is solid and strong, giving the young person the ability to:

- *be self-reliant,*
- *practice ethics and integrity,*
- *act with confidence and courage,*
- *have the ability not to take herself or himself too seriously,*
- *feel lovable and feel loved,*
- *take responsibility for self-initiated actions,*
- *approach life without fear,*
- *value her or his true Self,*
- *think independently of peer pressure,*
- *live by principle,*
- *seek counsel,*
- *make life decisions wisely, and*
- *face mistakes without falling apart.*

These (and other) characteristics, attributes, and attitudes make it possible to *have oneself off one's hands.* This means having the freedom to empathize with another person and be there for that person without interference by preoccupation with *me.* The confidence that comes from having an emotional core that is intact makes this freedom possible.

During the Vietnam War a study was conducted about the men at the front, the ones who faced the most grueling, difficult situations. Those who were doing the research found that there were two distinct groups: the men who could not function well under the pressure and those who did function well, even under the most trying circumstances. The research, focusing on finding out why some did well and some did not, revealed a definite pattern.

The men who could not function well broke down, acted carelessly, used drugs, and some went insane or deserted. It was generally found that the men who could not adapt well had endured childhood family experiences that would today be called dysfunctional. Some had been abused and deprived, abandoned in one way or another, and generally felt worthless. Many had been gang members, minor criminals, and drifters. These men had suffered a decided lack of tender loving care of their emotional core.

The men who did well under the most trying circumstances came from stable, loving homes. They had grown up feeling loved and honored as worthwhile individuals. Most of these men had never been addicted to drugs, did not have criminal records, and probably felt a sense of purpose and responsibility to themselves and others. Their emotional core was intact, or nearly so.

The common thread throughout each group was the type of childhood family experiences the men had known. A loving, supportive family background made a crucial difference in whether or not a man had a strong and solid emotional core.

If an emotional core in excellent condition could be pictured, it would probably look something like this:

If a damaged emotional core could be pictured, it might look something like one of these examples:

Even parents who are driven by their own emotional baggage, their search for ego fulfillment, or their own convenience, might govern the family very differently if they could see and understand what may be going on for the children. A lovely young woman came to our study group a few years ago, hoping to avoid a divorce. She invited us to her home, and we clearly saw that the children were suffering. We saw, too, that this woman's own injured emotional core blocked her ability to see and understand solutions and to implement ways to help her and her husband prevent divorce. The divorce took place, and she wrote to us later, "I never, never would have gone through with the divorce if I'd known how painful it would be for the kids and how adversely they would be affected. I know now that we could have worked it out, but now it is too late."

An Invisible Resource

Unfortunately, we do not live in an ideal world, and there are situations and circumstances where the emotional core of all family members cannot be perfectly protected and nourished at the same time. Choices have to be made and sometimes none of the choices are good ones. But life does not come to a halt to allow us to function in limbo, so we must move forward in the best way we can, balancing the options and choosing the ones that are the least harmful to the well-being of all family members and the family as a whole. Only the parents, however, have the maturity to become aware that the condition of their emotional core is getting in the way of family harmony. They are the ones who can reach for a higher, more objective level of guidance.

Even if we, as parents, are doing our part for our children, we have to remember that there are influences on them over which we have no control. These outside influences can bruise, injure, or damage their emotional core. However, if we make *every* effort to do our best to protect and nourish our children at home, they will meet these outside occurrences better than would otherwise have been possible, thus minimizing or possibly preventing any emotional core injuries. If an emotional core is damaged, it can heal, so no one need feel hopeless if damage has taken place.

One important preventive measure is not to send your children, at any stage of their childhood, out into the world too soon. It is often premature parental enthusiasm that causes a great portion of the injuries that occur to the emotional core of children. What may seem so easy to an adult is often uncomfortable or even traumatic for a child. What parents think will be good for a child, often is not. Parents can learn to see the world from their children's point of view, and at the same time, discard their own personal agendas that they would like to see fulfilled through the children. It is so simple to wait. There is a high future cost associated with pushing children ahead of their own personal timeline. Is it really necessary and wise that your little child of five years play soccer with the community team? What about all those other activities? Understanding and providing what your children *really* need may often mean acting counter to the culture, but may be the best way you can show them your love.

Consider giving your children a choice with no bias from you pressuring their decision. Make activities—whether sports or lessons or social events—optional. This simple solution is usually overlooked because there is an insistent belief in the culture that capability in a child automatically means readiness and interest. Another unfortunate belief is that children should be busy nearly every moment actively learning or achieving. That belief is actually counter to productive learning or achieving. Children of all ages need to rest and play.

Children thrive when they are given time to explore and then quietly enjoy each stage they go through. Let them walk on, on their own, instead of pushing or dragging them to the next stage or level. Children are born with curiosity and a desire to learn. Unfortunately, this enthusiasm is so often lost because of premature pressures that turn off their curiosity and joy of learning. What is the hurry? In our culture, children are, in general, being mercilessly rushed through childhood. Their lives are so crammed with stress and pressure that their right to a joyful childhood is lost. After all, children today can look forward to a lifetime of about one hundred years. There is no reason to rush them through their childhood. Give childhood back to your children. This is the best way to insure a healthy emotional core.

With *awareness* and *attention* you can create situations that will nourish and protect your children:

✧ Praise and show them that you appreciate them.
✧ Give children plenty of time to move from one stage to another *at their own pace.*
✧ Strive to demonstrate to them how valuable you feel they are; weigh all family decisions in the light of the effect those decisions have on the emotional core.
✧ Discourage any competitive activities before sufficient maturity takes place to make it possible for the children to handle the competition without stress.
✧ Positively reinforce children, verbally and nonverbally, many more times than you correct them.
✧ Remind your children frequently that you're glad they came to live with you, for no other reason than that they are very special individuals.
✧ See to it the children laugh many times a day.

✧ Give your children as many opportunities as possible to have control over some part of their lives.

✧ Separate mistakes and unacceptable behavior from the wonderful individuals that children *really* are. "You are wonderful, but that behavior is unacceptable."

✧ *Help children save face*, rather than facing humiliation.

Children can feel humiliated very easily. Often some of the remarks that are casually said to them are actually verbal abuse, unintentionally inflicted, but nevertheless injurious to the emotional core.

"How could you have done such a stupid thing?"

"You don't know *what* you want!"

"You're always getting into things!"

"NO! I'm too busy."

"You're so messy!"

"Why can't you ever do anything right?"

"You're an embarrassment to me."

"You are so mean."

"You look like a pig!"

"I'm ashamed to have you as my son."

To parents, statements such as these may seem to be just harmless expressions of exasperation, but to a child, these remarks are the emotional equivalent of a slap. Taking the time to give attention to a child's feelings is one of the wisest investments parents and other caregivers can make. A good principle is: *put yourself in the child's place.* How would *you* feel if someone were speaking to you (in a context that would fit your situation) with the words you just said to your child? "Can't you ever keep this house clean? "You're so clumsy!" "Are you eating—again?"

It is important to realize that caring for the emotional core does not preclude setting limits, making corrections, demanding family cooperation (including good manners), and requiring responses and behavior in keeping with principles. "Yes, Amy, I know you are frustrated, but hitting your brother is not allowed."

An Invisible Resource

We invite you to keep a running list of ideas of how to give tender loving care to the emotional core of your children. Start a list of those ideas that would be *specific for each one of your children.* Keep the list handy so you can add to it as you make additional observations. You may find this list to be a great help during the moments when there is no time to stop and figure it all out. "Amy, you have done a great job of trying. I'm so proud of you."

It is difficult to examine or measure a child's emotional core. Yet that emotional core begs for the most considerate and tender love, care, nourishment, and support from the adult world. Other children are not mature enough to help, so children can only depend on adults for this care. When the emotional core is intact and functioning from its inherent purity and beauty, your child has a priceless invisible resource for living.

8.

THE LITTLE PRINCESS

LILITA WAS TWO WHEN HER FATHER TOOK HER TO HIS PARENTS, Lilita's grandparents, hoping they would care for her. He realized that he had made a mistake when, in a moment of passion, he married Lilita's mother. His parents had been right. The marriage was neither a good nor a happy one. Lilita's mother had turned out to be slovenly, lazy, and alcoholic.

Lilita's grandparents were thrilled to have her, and Lilita grew up believing that *they* were her parents. She loved their beautiful home, her lovely bedroom with the canopy bed, and her many pretty dresses that each had matching ribbons for her hair. Lilita's parents (grandparents) often hugged her, held her on their laps, told her marvelous stories, and admired her creativity and artistic abilities. They set limits, gave her chores, and taught her good manners, yet they always listened when she talked and were proud of her brilliant way of expressing herself. Lilita's Mommy and Daddy often called her Our Little Princess and lovingly treated her like one.

This happy little family lived on a country estate in Mexico. Lilita's mother maintained a small grocery store at the side of the road so her neighbors wouldn't have to go all the way to town for things they may have forgotten or suddenly needed. Lilita remembers that she loved helping her mother in the store.

One day when Mommy went into the house for awhile, Lilita looked around for a new idea to make the store more beautiful to surprise Mommy.

She spotted the sacks of beans and beside them the sacks of rice. She thought, "If the brown beans and the white rice were mixed together instead of being all by themselves in the sacks, they would look much prettier." So mix them she did and proudly waited for Mommy to return.

When Mommy came back to the store she told Lilita that mixing the beans and rice had been such a lovely, creative idea, and they looked so much prettier. But she lovingly explained that they couldn't leave them that way because the customers wanted to buy rice and beans separately. Even though her Mommy must have gulped in dismay, she honored Lilita's creativity and valued her feelings more than the time, effort, and money it must have taken to rectify Lilita's work of art. Lilita remembers only love, no anger at all, and in no way was she made to feel guilty or rebuffed, hurt or reprimanded. The next day when there were again sacks of separated beans and rice in the store, she knew they must now remain separated, but didn't feel that she'd done a terrible thing the day before. Her emotional core was intact.

Lilita remembers her entire time with Mommy and Daddy as a time in which she was continually loved, praised, valued, and honored. She knows there were times she had to be corrected, but she doesn't remember any time that they spoke harshly or that she felt fear. (These people should have given parenting classes!)

Life was loving and joyful for the three of them until Lilita was in her seventh year. Then her Daddy died. She was devastated, but her Mommy was so inconsolable Lilita believes she must have suffered a nervous breakdown. In a few days a strange man came to the door. He asked her name, and when she replied, "Lilita," he announced, "I am your father." Lilita thought he was making a cruel joke and replied that her Daddy was dead. But this man was, indeed, Lilita's father, and he had come to take her away with him. She remembers her Mommy cried when the time came to say good-bye. Lilita couldn't understand. Why had Mommy let her go? There were no explanations that made sense to her. She could only cry during the hours she and her father were riding the train.

Lilita discovered that her new home was a one-room hovel off an alley. Her mother barely acknowledged her presence. There were two younger children and obviously another baby on the way. Everything was filthy, and the place smelled terrible. There was only one lumpy, dirty bed for all of them. Lilita's father now drank with his wife, and drifted from job to job. When there was no food or liquor left, he would go out for a day, beg some work, and they would eat awful food again for awhile.

Lilita soon realized she was no one's princess anymore, and there was no one to rescue her. She still thought of herself as a princess, but now, a displaced princess. She knew it was not her fault that she was suddenly thrown into such trying circumstances. Lilita was Cinderella during the bleak time before her fairy godmother came to take her to the ball, but there was an important difference: Lilita already knew she was a princess; Cinderella had to become one. Lilita's grandparents had already shown her their appreciation for her value as a person, as well as their appreciation for her creativity, innovation, and skillful thinking. More importantly, they helped her develop an appreciation of herSelf and her own resources. Of course, at seven a little girl would not *consciously* think about the value of Self and her resources, but these treasures were so much a part of her emotional core and consciousness that she never lost them.

In his drunken rages, Lilita's father often beat her and her siblings. Even as the beatings hurt, she always thought it was so stupid of him, and knew the harsh treatment didn't have anything to do with her. The abuse was more difficult for her two younger siblings; they took it personally. Her mother never defended the children, telling them over and over that their father was right. Lilita never believed it. She already knew her inherent value as a person.

Before the baby was born, her father went to the United States to see if the family could start a new life where his cousin was living in California. Weeks went by, the baby was born, and then more weeks went by without a word from their father. When the money he had left was about to run out, her desperate mother went off to find him.

Lilita did not panic when she was left alone to care for herself and the three younger children. "I can handle this," she said to herself. She didn't know how, but after all, she was a princess—a displaced princess—but a princess nevertheless. Lilita kept her confidence and did not despair.

Lilita's mother had been nursing the baby when she left and hadn't thought to leave any substitute provision. Lilita's creative and innovative abilities, the ones that had been so valued and honored by her grandparents, helped her provide for the baby. She confidently figured out that if she tore strips of material from one of her pretty dresses— still packed in a box—cooked up a gruel of rice, and soaked the material in it, the baby could suck on that. It worked!

Weeks passed before her parents came and took them all to the United States. The change didn't matter much to Lilita, because the conditions there were not much better. Her parents were still drunk most of the time. There was always enough liquor for them to drink, but rarely enough food for the children to eat.

As Lilita endured her life, she realized that the best way for her to get out of this terrible situation was to learn English perfectly and to get as good an education as she possibly could. She tried to interest her siblings in striving for themselves, but they didn't seem to care. Eventually there were nine children, eight girls and one boy. Conditions deteriorated even more at home, and finally Lilita found a job and an apartment of her own. She invited her siblings to live with her, and all except her brother joined her. She managed to help her older sisters get work and the young ones enroll in school. There were countless difficulties. More than once she had to seek foster homes for the children, but she kept striving, and would manage to create a new home and gather her sisters together again. She never gave up or gave in.

This went on for some years, and then Lilita fell in love and married. Later a daughter was born. It was soon obvious that this young husband's emotional core was in very bad shape. When everything was fine, life went smoothly, but at every challenge, he became domineering and abusive. At one point he kidnapped their daughter and they disappeared. Still, Lilita never gave up. She knew she could figure this out, too, and after three years she found them. With great confidence she confronted her daughter's father: "You have had her long enough, now it is my turn." She helped her daughter pack up her belongings and they left. The man never protested and never bothered her again. She was able to take charge because the message from her emotional core kept silently reminding her, "You are valuable and deserving and you can do it."

The Little Princess

After being taken from her grandmother, she faced many difficult challenges, but she always met them as a little princess. Her eight siblings were not so fortunate. Her brother spent time in prison and none of her sisters were able to create truly successful lives, except as they were carried along on Lilita's wings and shared her success. What was the difference in the capabilities of these siblings? The difference between her attitude and the attitudes of her siblings was a result of the condition of her emotional core compared to theirs.

Lilita planned strategically until she was able to open her own very successful small business. As a single working mother she raised two lovely daughters as princesses, and now she has married a fine man who values her as a queen.

Lilita would like to tell her grandparents, "Thank you, Grandmother and Grandfather, for showing me I am a valuable Princess."

9.

SPECIAL PARENTING TOOLS

Win: The children were about four and seven when we launched the family consciously into practicing principles. Bill had been trained as an engineer, so his mind automatically followed a principle path. I quickly saw that his way of solving problems, whether furnace troubles in our home or design problems at work, always followed the principle path and always worked. However, we were overwhelmed at first with parenting and just blundered along with rules and principles without giving too much thought about which was which. Engineers don't take a course, Principles in Parenting 101, so it didn't occur to Bill for several years to use the principle path consciously in our daily life unless, of course, he was fixing the furnace. Finally we realized that life with the family would go much more smoothly if we were serious about using principles in our parenting.

THE PRINCIPLE PATH

WE TALKED AND PLANNED TOGETHER, and then included the children in our discussions about principles. We carefully explained the universal truth of principles with examples, such as "If you put your hand on a hot stove, you'll get burned." We explained the principle of gravity by throwing a rock over a cliff. We noticed the children didn't walk so close to the edge after that. We illustrated the principle of 2 + 2 = 4 by gathering many objects and showing that adding two of any item to two of another item or to two of the same item *always* resulted in a total of four. Our examples illustrated one of the important points of the definition of a principle as we used the word: a principle applies in every case and for everyone. *Everyone* who falls over a cliff will fall to the bottom; some won't fly into the sky. Everyone who adds two items to two more items will have four items. We began with these simple examples of principles, and progressed to much more complex principles. We also explained the possibility of flexibility in the use of some principles, for instance, the principle of courtesy can be used in many different ways.

Principles were the most valuable and effective tools we discovered in our long search for parenting help; they provided a guidance system we could rely on with confidence. Over time we developed some clear understanding and guidelines to follow.

What is a principle?

✧ A fundamental, *universal* truth, for example,
the law of gravity, 2 + 2 = 4

✧ A guideline for conduct of living, which is based on a
fundamental, universal truth, for example, the principles of
freedom, orderliness, balance, and respect

Practicing principles, *as we use the word,* will not violate integrity. However, the word *principle* is sometimes used otherwise. For example, a thief might say he is living by a principle that we would judge not to be a principle because it *does* violate integrity: "Steal all that I can and not get caught."

PRINCIPLES VS. RULES

There are two ways to govern a family: one way is to discover and implement principles based on universal wisdom and the other way is to make up rules as problems occur. Principles are more impersonal than rules, because they are based on truths that have been discovered, not preferences made up by the parent. Principles create an attitude of functioning well together as a family. Rules usually have a personal, arbitrary connotation of one person controlling another, which engenders feelings of resistance and resentment, pulling down the family atmosphere.

What is a rule?

✧ A mandate, law, or regulation prescribed by persons, organizations, or the culture to control conduct or action, for example, traffic laws

A *rule* is generally considered to be an order, personally and arbitrarily decided upon and fixed by a person(s) in order to control or regulate the behavior, actions, and/or general life of another or others. In contrast, a *principle* is generally considered to be an impersonal truth, or wisdom.

Soon after we discovered principles as valuable parenting tools, we examined the rules we had set up to govern the household. We found some of the household rules were actually principles. We saved those principles for our family use, then threw out the others that were just rules. It worked like magic! Attitudes changed, tension lessened, and daily family living became much simpler. We were delighted that after eliminating rules, the picky corrections and comments that often spoiled a moment were eliminated. Uncontrolled emotional experiences were reduced, mistakes were avoided, and decisions were easier to make. Switching from a rule-centered home to a principle-centered home gave the family more time for fun and more room for an atmosphere of joy.

One of the arbitrary rules that we discarded had to do with jackets: the children must wear jackets *if we decided* it was cold enough. We gave them the news, "From now on we're not taking the responsibility for your being warm enough outdoors. You are free to choose when to wear your jackets." They were pleased to be honored as having sense enough to know when they were cold.

Win: *I nearly bit off the end of my tongue the first few days, because the habit was so strong to tell the children when to wear*

their jackets. In reality, how did I know when they were cold? They were running around far more than I would have. I noticed the children often dashed outside and then came in to get their jackets. It was a nice freedom not to have to think any more about the jacket issue.

All of us used the word *principle* regularly and naturally in daily living. We reminded the children a thousand times (according to them) "You will either live by principles or by suffering." At first *we* made the list of family principles we wanted to use to govern our home and explained them to the children. But, as the children matured, they contributed to the list as well. Sometimes we started with an incident and then searched for the principle that would apply to it. At other times we started with a basic principle, for example, *courtesy.* Then we talked about applying it to various situations. In the case of courtesy, one application applied to complaints. All family members were welcome to make any complaints they wished, but making them politely was strongly encouraged.

WHAT IS THE PRINCIPLE?

Bill: To help Jill and Jim understand the abstract concept of principles, we looked for opportunities for them to discover for themselves some principles from the physical world. One time when we were traveling, the car ahead of us had a bouncy rear tire. We drove behind that car for many miles while the children and I discussed why the tire was bouncing and which principles would have to be applied in order to fix it. In addition, we explored a large variety of subjects. How do bicycles, skis, airplanes, and mixers work? How do seeds produce flowers? What makes bridges stand up? What causes the sun to disappear every night? The question always was, What are the principles? We all enjoyed these discussions, and they helped the children develop an interest and a skill in finding principles.

By inference, we built on the idea that just as the successful structure of a car or a house or a bicycle is based on principles, lives of individuals and families also run more smoothly if those lives are built on a structure of principles.

Win: Not long after the children understood the principle concept, Jill was teaching Jim how to roller skate. I saw that she was talking to him, but I couldn't hear what she was saying. I did observe, however, that Jim kept falling down. Then Jill raised her voice to a motherly pitch and said firmly, "Jim, if you would just concentrate and listen to me, I'll give you the principles of skating and you won't fall down."

Jill lowered her voice, and while standing over him as he was sprawled on the patio, apparently explained to him the principles of skating. I saw Jim get up, take off, and he didn't fall again. Learning the principles made an immediate and dramatic change in his roller skating. We always enjoyed watching the children realize that living by principles works.

PRINCIPLES AND CONSEQUENCES

Intrinsic to a principle are both the positive results of living by the principle and the consequences of violating the principle. Adults usually see this point easily, but because so many consequences are subtle or occur at a future time, children often have difficulty understanding that the consequences of violating a principle are intrinsic to the principle itself. Once children have touched a hot stove, they probably won't do it again, but most principles and their consequences aren't so obvious.

Children violate principles, not because they are plotting to do so or want to do something wrong, but because they simply do not have the maturity to pay attention on a consistent basis. When we saw this effect of immaturity, we knew it would be kinder to the children and easier for us to get their attention if we developed a set of attention-getters, or artificial consequences. When a principle was violated—depending on the nature of the principle—the intrinsic consequence was immediately realized or the artificial consequence was immediately and with detachment, invoked. For example, placing the children on a chair for a few minutes was an artificial consequence to get their attention and give them the opportunity to focus on the violated principle. However, "Go to your room!" was never a consequence. We wanted Jill and Jim to feel positive about their rooms as a haven and sanctuary, places more intimate than the whole house.

When the children were mature enough, the consequences and the artificial consequences of violating principles were made clear in advance. Jill and Jim, themselves, often decided what consequence would apply. Having in place predetermined attention-getting consequences kept the situation impersonal. Then it became the children's decision whether or not to honor the principles.

When we established a structure of principles to live by and the consequences to trigger attention to remember the principles, problems were resolved quickly and easily, without fear and uncertainty on our part and without resentment on the part of the children. This improvement over rules was achieved because we all knew the *principles* were the governing authority of the household.

The accumulation of experience over time proved to the children that you do either live by principles or by suffering. Living by suffering is the hard way. It was heartening when the children began to see this point in real life situations. When Jill was about ten, she told us one of her girlfriends had been having difficulty handling an unpleasant incident in her life. Jill declared, "It's stupid to learn the hard way, she should find the principle."

• *Principles generally are uniformly beneficial to all concerned, even though everyone concerned may not think so.*
• *The violation of principles results in consequences.*

• *Rules are often primarily beneficial to the one who created the rule.*
• *The violation of rules results in punishment.*

Using the words, *consequences* and *punishment*, properly is important. Words, themselves, can become wings or prison bars. These word pairs are a good example:

The word pairs, *principle* and *consequence,* and *rule* and *punishment,* carry two important different connotations in our culture, and therefore, elicit two different results:

1. The response to *principles* and *consequences* is receptivity.
2. The reaction to *rules* and *punishment* is resistance and resentment.

We all know that obeying rules can often seem to have positive results, but obeying is often simply conforming in order to avoid punishment. Therefore, *rules* and *punishment* incur fear, resentment, and the desire to avoid punishment. In our experience *principles* and *consequences* usually don't invoke this negative reaction because of their universal impersonal nature.

"It Can Happen to Me"

Practicing principles makes it possible to avoid many tragic mistakes in our unforgiving world. For example, so many of our precious young people have been seriously injured or killed by violating the principle: *It is foolish to drink and drive.* Why do young people, who have heard this principle many times, get caught in the trap, "Oh, it won't happen to me"? We believe they may not have been given the opportunity to find out that principles do apply to them, and that consequences *can* happen to them even though they are good and nice people.

Too often during the growing years young people have encountered no serious consequences for violations of principles. Teachers, friends, parents, and relatives intervene and prevent the consequences from occurring. "We know you aren't supposed to drive the car for two months if you cause any damage, but that fender isn't bad, and I know you didn't mean it." "We know you're not supposed to have a sleep-over if your science project isn't finished, but you've worked hard, so go ahead." There are appropriate times to practice flexibility within the principle. But the repeated *intervention,* when the principle and the violation are known, sets up a dangerous pattern and a mistaken expectation. This intervention gives young people the idea that principles are forgiving and don't need to be respected. Then when a young person is tempted to violate a principle and there is no one around who cares and would intervene, the learned reaction jumps into place, "Oh, I needn't worry, nothing bad can happen to me."

If children and young people can learn to respect principles in situations that mean a lot to them but aren't dangerous, they will build a respect for principles in all situations. With this respect they can build their own set of principles by their own process of learning and observing that the violation of principles can and often does result in serious consequences for themselves and others.

PRINCIPLES AND FEAR

Just as knowing that violating principles does result in consequences is important, knowing that love is not a substitute for principles is also important. There is a belief in our culture that love eliminates fear. However, this belief has never been convincingly substantiated. When we have examined lives of individuals, couples, families, and groups, we have observed an abundance of love present in the individual and in the relationships, yet fear is not curtailed. Love can be a comforting agent, but we have not seen love, in and of itself, eliminate fear. This is painfully obvious in the parent-child relationship. Fear is usually a close companion to love and the fear drives much of the parenting experience, which generates fear in the children. This is an unstable relationship. We have heard parents say, "If we just keep loving enough everything will be all right." When everything is not all right, however, the parents assume that they are not loving enough and fear continues to govern the relationship. It is possible, however, to eliminate fear. We eliminate fear from our lives and our children's lives as we adopt and live by principles.

APPLYING PRINCIPLES

As Jill and Jim became more mature, we continued to explore the principles behind the obvious. We discussed many principles, including freedom, identity, relationships, and balance and how they applied to various aspects of the human scene, such as politics, choices, dating, and employment. During Jill's college years, she dated a young man whose family lived in Oregon. She was invited to visit his family during one of the holidays. At that time she thought she and her boyfriend might eventually marry, so meeting the family was important. She asked us for some principles she could use during the visit to help accomplish her investigation of the family background.

We met the challenge, and wrote "Meeting the Family," the beginning of a handbook for our "Preparation for Marriage" course. The four of us met at Jill's college apartment and discussed the ideas that we'd gathered, and Jill and Jim added many more. After the trip Jill told us she put "Meeting the Family" right on top of her suitcase so she could frequently check it for ideas. The principles alerted her to areas that she may not have otherwise noticed or considered important. For instance, the family used language far more coarse than she wanted used in her future home. Although we guessed, from what we'd seen and heard, that the relationship wasn't a good match, Jill discovered the mismatch on her own by applying the principles of exploration to the various determining factors, such as background, goals and interests, priorities, and the condition of the emotional core.

As Jill and Jim became young adults, we were excited to watch them spreading their wings and flying off with the principle of using principles. One of the reasons Jim chose to be an engineer was that he enjoys knowing how things work. When things don't work, he enjoys finding the principles to fix them. Jim called us one day from college and shared that he'd been struggling for several days to figure something out. We've forgotten the exact subject, but we remember him saying that the frustration was driving him nuts. Then he added with exhilaration, "Finally I found the principle and everything fell into place!"

> *Bill: I like the axiom, "It's better to teach a man how to fish, than to give him a fish." When Jim told us this story, we felt we had, indeed, taught him how to fish, so he never need be hungry.*

Jill also chose a career in which knowing and using principles is a central theme. She studied Computer Science and enjoyed many professional years as a software engineer before changing careers to become a full-time Mom.

Principles as parenting tools were special to us in four ways:

1 Our knowledge of principles gave us guidance in which we could have consistent confidence.

2 Our use of principles to resolve problems in family life eliminated struggling in contests of wills.

3 Through the family experience our children developed the skill of finding and using principles for their own independent lives.

4 Parenting by principle was parenting by wisdom, not by fear.

The freedom that results from parenting with principles is truly amazing. Everyone wins—joyfully!

10.

A Treasure Chest of Tools

L IVING BY PRINCIPLES FACILITATES that special way of parenting—
living joyfully with children. We are grateful to have discovered
and then used many valuable principles. Based on our experience
in living with these principles as a family we have selected and gathered into this treasure chest *some* of the best, most effective ones in
our collection. We have written these principles in a form that will
make them easy to apply in family situations, but you may wish to
customize many of them so they will be most effective for your family.

✧ *A household filled with joy creates an atmosphere where
family harmony flourishes.*

✧ *Parenting by fear may be very effective at the moment, but guiding
with wisdom is much more effective in the long run.*

✧ *Parents who nourish their own relationship enrich their
children's lives.*

✧ *Instead of over-directing, allow children to make their own
discoveries and solve their own problems.*

✧ *Corrections are best made in the form of a sandwich: two thick
slices of praise and reinforcement with a thin filling of gentle correction that addresses the behavior or mistake, and is not a criticism of
the child as a person.*

✧ Wise parents never take it personally when their children are angry at them. It is impossible to think clearly and wisely in the state of taking things personally.

✧ Children's rooms should be their sanctuary—a place they look forward to occupying with a feeling of safety, comfort, and pleasure. Sending children to their rooms as a consequence or as punishment spoils the benefit of this important refuge.

✧ The condition of a child's emotional core, even though invisible, plays a major role in the child's entire life.

✧ The word, principle, is a natural part of an enlightened family's vocabulary.

✧ Using food as a bribe, punishment, or comfort may be expeditious at the moment, but can set up conditions that may be regretted in the future. If following this principle results in unbearable crying or yelling, get ear plugs.

✧ Look behind misbehavior. It is usually based on fear.

✧ Privacy and individual quiet time for each member of the family is important every day. Children and adults constantly on-the-go cannot grow deep roots of emotional strength.

✧ If parents expect that their children will naturally be disobedient, they surely will be disobedient. This principle may apply to other expectations as well.

✧ Sometimes being bored is the only way children can experience an "empty space" in their lives in which to be creative and develop the ability to think.

✧ The parents' attitudes and belief systems about life are directly transmitted to children—even if never spoken.

✧ Children should not be asked, "Why did you do that?" In answer to that question, have you ever heard a toddler say, "Well, I tell you, Mom, I really wanted to take the Kool-aid into the family room, but I didn't know I wasn't mature enough to do it without spilling"? The child doesn't know why; the question creates a sense of inadequacy and fear.

✧ *Replace fear in the family with principle and experience family freedom.*

✧ *The bond between child and parent is natural and necessary, but it is a binding. Parents are responsible to loosen those bindings, starting in small ways when the child is small, so both freedom and responsibility can gradually develop.*

✧ *Unnecessary stress in the household can be prevented by being flexible within principle.*

✧ *A family creates happy memories as activities are enjoyed together that are imaginative, fun, and unexpected—for example, a picnic indoors on a rainy day, eating cake for breakfast, painting a mural on the garage wall.*

✧ *What children experience, see, and hear, even when they are too young to intellectually understand, can become lifelong patterns of attitude and behavior. These patterns can be negative or positive: for example, patterns of foul language and anger, or patterns of gentleness and joyfulness.*

✧ *Every parent and every child is doing the best she or he can at any particular moment. Hopefully, the next "moment" will be better.*

✧ *There are many events that take place, even in a child's first year, that will contribute to the kind of life a family has together when that child is a teenager. Instead of dreading the teens, begin to invest NOW to make the teen years positive for your family.*

✧ *Children who are completely in charge of their school homework develop responsibility and self-confidence.*

✧ *Supporting children must be balanced with avoiding unnecessary interference in their lives.*

✧ *In the case of adult children, biting one's tongue when unsolicited advice starts to slip out can be uncomfortable, but certainly avoids problems.*

✧ *Every individual is inherently valuable. Every individual longs to have that inherent value recognized and appreciated.*

✧ *Let children learn; whenever possible refrain from teaching them.*

✧ *Choose your issues carefully, otherwise you lose all effectiveness when it's most needed.*

✧ *Learn not to take things personally so hurt feelings, fear, emotional stress, and misunderstandings can be avoided. This is an important lesson for everyone in the family.*

✧ *Consciously providing relaxation avoids a multitude of problems and promotes physical, mental, and emotional harmony for the family.*

✧ *Parenting partners who support each other's parenting actions build their children's sense of security. Have a standing agreement to resolve in private differences over parenting decisions.*

✧ *Giving complete attention when a child talks to you supports the child's awareness of Self-value.*

✧ *Family fun and laughter every day is just as important as brushing teeth—maybe more important.*

Enjoy discovering and adding additional principles to the Treasure Chest, thereby creating your own unique list of family principles. You will find living by principles is an exciting and rewarding family adventure.

11.

THIS IS A
MUSEUM

PICTURE THE FIRST TIME your toddler opens the cabinet under the kitchen sink. Just think what a triumph that little one feels when she or he is first able to open those doors! You don't want to dampen that feeling of success, but you are prepared. You gently take hold of those little arms reaching out and say, with no tension, anger, impatience, or yelling, "That is a museum in there, Sweetheart. A museum is a looking place, not a touching or grabbing place. Just look, don't touch." You stand there, repeating the words, and holding the child's arms until the straining to wrench free is relaxed. It is important that the child be allowed to look as long as she or he desires. Then carry on the same process again and again each time your child reaches out.

> **Win:** *The first time our grandson, Ryan, discovered the cupboard under the kitchen sink, Bill did this twenty-eight times with a relaxed, loving attitude and gently spoken words. When Ryan realized his repeated tries were not getting him anywhere, he went elsewhere. Ryan discovered the bathroom cupboard next. I held his arms and spoke gently and lovingly, "That is a museum in there, just look, don't touch." This took place seventeen times before he turned to do something else. We first introduced the museum principle when Ryan was eleven months; now at twenty-six months, he knows and respects the tempting places in the house designated as museums. He explores by looking, not touching.*

This is a Museum

We were careful to remove poisonous or valuable items, and we gated off the living room. At first, we concentrated just on the cupboards and drawers that Ryan could open. Overdoing the choice of areas designated as museums is unkind, therefore, don't be tempted to make the entire house a museum and everything in it museum pieces. Keep a realistic balance.

Even though you know your child isn't yet able to understand you intellectually, accompany the physical limits you are setting with gentle words explaining the concept. The words and the actions both help the concept to gradually become a part of the child's consciousness.

We call this Loving Learning, which is learning in an atmosphere where the child feels complete acceptance as a valued and appreciated person. There is no fear present in this atmosphere. Loving Learning supports joyful family living, and it is the most effective learning possible for children of all ages.

There is another way of learning—fear, humiliation, and punishment. While that way can be very effective in the short-term, it is counterproductive in the long-term because it is damaging to the emotional core and undermines the learning process. Another solution that doesn't involve learning at all, is to put everything out of reach and lock doors and drawers.

When Ryan occasionally forgets, we gently repeat: "This is a museum (or museum piece). Just look and don't touch," sometimes holding his arms while he looks. This is always done with kindness, relaxation, patience, and acceptance of the true Self of this individual.

If Ryan grabs something and starts walking with it, we gently guide him back to the cupboard and help him put it back saying, "Remember, Sweetie, all the things in there are museum pieces, just to look at, not to touch. Thank you for putting it back." Now we leave some fragile things out and the gate is gone. We trust him, while keeping alert. He intellectually understands more now what museum and museum piece mean, and when we say the words, he usually only looks.

Win: *Ryan tests the limits more when he knows we are watching than when he thinks he's completely on his own. This is where our special parental back eyes come in handy. We can act if necessary,*

or ignore if not, without disturbing the child. Once Ryan was play-
ing near some glass objects on display. He looked up at them and
then at me. I was nearby, but he didn't realize I could see him with
my back eyes. He looked at the glass briefly before going back to
his play. He didn't touch.

Children don't have to touch, pick up, grab, throw, or trash everything in sight. Our own experience and experiences of other families
prove that grabbing and throwing isn't something programmed into
the genes but rather an expectation of the culture. All through life
there are certain objects to be treated only as museum pieces, and it is
actually easier for children if they learn early in life that sometimes
they may not touch, but they may look. They learn the museum principle before ever going to a museum, so there is no sudden stressful
learning curve when their world enlarges to include real museums,
other people's homes, and stores.

Three important principles of Loving Learning are:

1. Do not let anger, impatience, or exasperation in attitude, voice,
or action enter your consciousness.
2. Never use the resistance and fear-generating word, NO!
3. Shower praise on the children with hugs, smiles, and cheerful
words when they remember, but *don't* frown or punish when they forget. A cheerful attitude of "We'll try again later, Sweetie," works best.

Violating any of these principles will abort the Loving Learning
process.

A great investment of time, patience, attention, and repetition is
required to successfully implement the Loving Learning process. The
stunning results are certainly worth the effort.

Postscript: It is now over two years since this essay was written. In the
meantime, Ryan's sister, Deanna, has joined the family. Interestingly,
Deanna learned the museum principle very quickly, undoubtedly
because it was already established in the family's consciousness.

12.

No! No! No!

WHEN A LITTLE CHILD BEGINS to crawl and explore the world, the joy of that exploration is frequently spoiled by NO! NO! NO! This message comes verbally, and also non-verbally through spanking, slapping, yanking, and negative facial expressions. When children of the middle childhood and adolescent years attempt to venture out, they also frequently receive NO! NO! NO! in various ways.

We're not talking about a polite, gentle No, but rather the emotionally charged NO! that children experience from fearful, angry, or frustrated parents. The word, in and of itself, is not the culprit. It's the loaded reactions that are triggered when anyone in our culture hears that word. The cultural program goes something like this: "Whenever you tell me NO! I'm going to do my best to defy you." This pattern of parent-child conflict seems to be, at least in part, the root of the terrible twos, teenage rebellion, and obstinate adults.

When our first grandchild was expected, we thought a lot about the most positive role we could play as grandparents. One subject we talked about was the emotionally charged word, NO! We didn't want Ryan to hear this from us. We knew we would have to set some limits, but we wanted to set and enforce the limits without using NO! and causing a negative reaction in his consciousness. For the most part, we have acted according to the plan. But we have been amazed and dismayed to find the cultural NO! pattern such a strong influence that once in awhile the word will still come forth. Ryan's parents

also experience the same surprises. But, in general, we have all succeeded quite well in not using the emotionally charged word.

One of the common symptoms of the terrible twos is the frequent
and defiant "NO!" yelled by the child. However, we have never heard
it from Ryan. He does say, "No," sometimes, but it is spoken as a fact,
softly: "No eat," "No throw," "No," in answer to a question. Ryan is
thirty-three months now and is a sweet and cooperative little boy. He
vents frustration when his ideas can't be accommodated at the
moment, but he does not exhibit the typical terrible twos syndrome.

Parents are amazed when their toddler begins to repeatedly yell,
"NO!" But if they could observe themselves, they would realize they
taught the attitude and the word to the child. It's not something in
the genes. A child who is yelled at learns to yell. A child who is
spanked learns to hit. A child who is constantly thwarted becomes
rebellious. This kind of parental behavior generates fear, resentment,
and resistance in the child.

In most cases children hear "NO!" many, many times a day. They
come to think that's about all their parents have to say to them. Of
course, if a situation of sudden impending danger arises, it may be
necessary to yell, "NO!" to get a child's attention. If the child has not
continually heard that emotionally charged word, she or he is far
more likely to correctly and quickly respond.

Exploration must sometimes be thwarted, and limits must be set,
but this can be done without verbally or physically inflicting NO!
One excellent way to enforce limits without using NO! is to just
physically move a small child. Once when Ryan was about eighteen
months, he set his sights on a shelf of glass objects. His Dad immediately walked to him, picked him up, and deposited him in another
part of the room where something else caught his attention. All this
was done silently and gently, generating no fear in Ryan.

Firmly but kindly holding the child's arms while she or he visual-
ly explores forbidden objects is another way of handling potentially
hazardous curiosity. We usually accompany holding the child's arms
with gentle, loving patter that does not include NO! such as "That is
a museum piece, Sweetheart. Just look."

As children mature, there is another option available instead of
using the loaded word, NO! Parents can simply explain the reason an

action is not acceptable. For example, when Ryan would begin to handle something breakable or begin to play with the dishwasher control buttons, we would say, "That is not a toy, Sweetheart. We don't play with that because . . ." This changes the encounter from that of one person controlling another to pointing out a fact or a principle which applies to everyone in that situation. Then, the reason Ryan stops playing with the dishwasher buttons is not because he was told, "NO!" but because dishwasher buttons simply are not designed to be used as toys by anyone.

For children in the middle and teen years, continuing to avoid the use of NO! leads parents to bring up and discuss the principles that apply to the issue at hand.

Susie asks, "May I go to a movie tonight?"

Dad replies, "Our family has two principles that will answer that question. First, does the movie measure up to the family standards? Second, will your homework be finished before you go?"

Of course, the word *no* will continue to be used as part of normal conversation, but, hopefully, the use of NO! as a controlling word will have fallen away from your family interactions. No one likes to feel controlled, and certainly the children of the middle childhood years and the adolescents rebel against it with the greatest of resistance. Just say a controlling "NO!" and years of relationship building have flown out the window. Using NO! is too expensive. Fortunately, there are many ways to fulfill parenting responsibilities without using NO!

Watch yourself throughout the day: How many times does a "NO!" slip out of your mouth? Look at those times. Pick out areas that really must be off-limits, for example, the stove top in the kitchen for little children and discourteous behavior for the older ones. Enforce those limits gently, but firmly. Then good-naturedly tolerate infractions of the less important preferences, such as exploring a shelf of books or the use of harmless slang now and then. Your home will be much happier than it can be when NO! is a constant pattern of daily living.

13.

THE RHYTHM OF READINESS

THAT LAWN ISN'T MOWED YET!" When Jim was in high school, one of his family chores was mowing the lawn. We told him to watch the lawn and when it reached an agreed upon height, to mow it. He was very cooperative about doing the mowing, but great family tension developed about the timing of the mowing. We kept noticing the lawn getting higher and higher and Jim making no mention of, or movement toward, mowing it. He walked across the lawn twice a day going to and from school; why didn't he see the growing lawn? When we reminded him that the lawn needed mowing, he was perfectly willing to mow it at his next opportunity. We thought, of course, he should be able to see for himself when it needed to be mowed, and a reminder from us should not be necessary.

We were wrong. After contemplating the problem, we realized that Jim simply wasn't yet ready to handle that nuance of responsibility. We had been fooled because he *seemed* to be ready. But we were unreasonable to expect him to handle all the other responsibilities of his life, which he did well, and also keep track of something so unrelated to his personal concerns. When he went to school, his mind was on getting to school; when he came home, his mind was on getting into the house to do whatever he wanted to do next, such as, clean his fish tank, sometimes do homework, sometimes decorate his room. Looking down at the lawn and analyzing whether or not it needed mowing was not something he could do at that stage of his development. The problem had been our misjudgment, not his negligence. When we agreed that we would simply tell him when it was time to mow the lawn and that he would then do it within twenty-four hours, we had peace again. When we finally recognized his non-readiness on this particular issue, the problem was solved.

READINESS AND RHYTHM

One of the most valuable principles we discovered while we were actively parenting was the principle of *the rhythm of readiness. Every individual has a unique rhythm of readiness, which could also be called a personal timeline.* At first we thought in terms of readiness; later, the importance of rhythm came to us. We use the term rhythm to emphasize that, given sufficient time, a child repeatedly becomes ready for each successive stage of advancement. The rhythm of *getting ready — advancing, getting ready — advancing, getting ready — advancing,* can be likened to an orchestra conductor's one-two, one-two, one-two to set the pace with which the orchestra will play a particular piece of music.

Just as an orchestra looks to its conductor to set the pace for moving through the music, we realized that as parents we needed to look to each of the children to set the pace for moving through the melody of her or his childhood. A good orchestra does not get ahead of the conductor or lag behind. Similarly, we tried to be alert not to push advancement before the children gave a sign of readiness or fail to offer opportunities for advancement when the children became ready. But what was the perfect balance between those two elements? We often didn't know for sure, but we tried to learn how to listen. The best we could do was to adopt the policy that if we were to make an error, it was better to err on the side of letting the children rest in readiness rather than pushing them prematurely into advancing—the last thing we wanted to risk.

A little friend of ours, Emily, received a bike before she was emotionally ready to handle unexpected falls or complicated maneuvers, even though she was physically capable of riding the bike under perfect circumstances. After a few highly frustrating incidents for Emily which ended in tears and frustration, she wanted nothing to do with the bike. Her mother was visibly upset and disappointed, and Emily interpreted her mother's reaction as disappointment *personally in her.*

But her mother was really disappointed in herself for getting Emily a bike too soon. Unfortunately, Emily wasn't mature enough to understand the real cause of her mother's agitation, and she suffered needlessly. Experiences like Emily's and her mother's weaken a child's emotional core and the strength of the family as a whole. Bike riding was premature. Waiting perhaps just a few months longer for the bike could have turned biking into a happy experience for Emily.

On the other hand, when children's rhythms are respected, the positive effect on their entire lives and on family harmony and joy is significant. As children are allowed and encouraged to progress in development according to the *intrinsic pattern of their own biological, emotional, mental, and spiritual timeline,* they are able to grow deep roots in consciousness that will provide strength and stability with which to meet the varied situations that arise in life.

READINESS AND NATURE'S PATTERN

Have you ever observed children and commented to yourself, "They're being robbed of their childhood"? We do. Children who are expected to be reading books at five or six, who are forced to take almost complete care of themselves at eight, or who have no time after school to do what they want at any age, aren't experiencing childhood as nature intended. The current expectations and pressures of our society are pushing children off balance far beyond their rhythm of readiness.

We see children who are burned out by the time they are eight or ten, but the parents of these children usually don't even notice their children are frazzled, and therefore, can do nothing to give them the space to recover. We adults know that when we are exhausted, *we* have little or no access to our personal strength. The same certainly applies to children. This is part of the reason that children often do not meet wisely or well crucial heavy demands on them when parents aren't around to help. Many children in today's cultural environment are required to care for themselves for long periods in ways far beyond their natural capacity. When worried parents, and society as a whole, wonder why their children, adolescents, and young adults have so many problems, there is generally a complete unawareness of the state of instability so often caused by violation of the rhythm of readiness for each child.

The Rhythm of Readiness

We viewed Jill and Jim as conductors of the orchestras of each of *their* lives, and tried to get ourselves into step with their readiness, rather than expecting *them* to be in step with us, the lawn, the neighborhood, and the entire culture. We parents can safely assume a child will walk, eat table food, begin to use the toilet, and learn to read and write. The big questions become: *When* is the time for table food? Look into her or his mouth; are the necessary molars there? *When* can I throw away the diapers? When the child understands the process and is ready to take on the responsibility, without stress, for getting to the toilet. *When* will the child be ready to learn to read? When that child personally feels the need and desire to do so.

READINESS AND THE WHOLE CHILD

We experienced a dynamic expansion of awareness when we realized that a child's readiness is a function of the *whole* child, including readiness in physical, mental, intellectual, and emotional areas.

The concept seems so simple, but is so elusive. We saw the readiness error so clearly in Emily's experience with the bike. Her mother realized that Emily had become a master on her trike and was sure she could pedal a two-wheeler just fine. But Emily wasn't emotionally ready to cope with the advanced demands of bike riding. Emily and her mother both suffered because of trying to proceed despite this lack of readiness.

We have observed that mental, intellectual, and emotional readiness often come later than physical readiness, but sometimes readiness is reversed. When Ryan was eight or nine months, we could tell he wanted so badly to walk. He wanted to explore. But his little legs weren't ready yet, so he had to wait a few months to fulfill his longing to explore.

READINESS AND LEARNING

One of the discoveries that excited us was that children innately love to learn. What happens, then, to spoil that enthusiasm? What does it take to preserve that eagerness? We learned the answers through an experience with our son, Jim.

During first grade Jim was part of a school experiment called open classrooms. In a large round building, there were separate classrooms with side walls part way to the ceiling. All of the rooms were open to the center community area. The basics were taught in the individual rooms, then the children would go to the center area or to other rooms for art, music, sharing, and story time. Going to school became torture for Jim, and his complaints about school accelerated.

> **Win:** *Jim came from his bedroom one morning and told me he couldn't go to school that day. He assured me he wasn't sick, and intuitively, I knew Jim just could not go to school for emotional reasons; he was being guided by his own consciousness to stay home. I trusted that, and he stayed home.*

In order to better understand the situation, I went to school with Jim for an entire day. A steady rumble echoed throughout the building most of the time. Every time a class moved to another area, the moving children chattered, distracting those who were supposed to be engrossed in reading or numbers. The piano was just on the other side of the partition of Jim's area, making it impossible for any group to concentrate during another class's music lesson. When the time came for Jim's class to move, the directions weren't clear and the kids wandered aimlessly before the teacher yelled to herd them into the right area. When we walked home for lunch, I wanted to quit, but I went back with Jim to finish the day. The noise and confusion continued until the closing bell.

After my day at school I could easily understand why Jim seemed drained and disturbed when he came home from school. He'd always been composed, but lively, alert, and inquisitive. We were upset to see this change in him. Even though we didn't have it figured out, we knew that something needed to be done.

Since there was no alternative within the system, we cast about for an answer that would make it possible for the injury that had occurred in Jim's emotional core to heal. Because I have a Life Elementary Credential for teaching in California the idea occurred to us that we could have school at home. We proposed the idea to both Jill and Jim, suggesting that if they wanted to try learning at home, we would do so one year at a time. They went off to Jill's room, conferred, and made a list of the pros and cons. When they came to us after their consultation, they carried a long list of pros and only one con, and that one had been crossed out. Their only concern had been not being able to play with their friends during the school hours, but when they realized they didn't really play with their friends until *after* school, anyway, that concern dissolved. Jill and Jim wanted to try school at home.

So we began, hoping that our home-based schooling would allow Jim's bruised emotional core to heal. We didn't create a school environment, but were flexible and casual. Jim's first grade experience had been so unpleasant that he was not interested in academics at all, so this flexible atmosphere suited him just fine. We decided not to push him, because we knew children are naturally eager to learn.

Jill was eager to study, and chose subjects that interested her and had a wonderful time. We called our home-based schooling, Expansion, and she certainly expanded. Later she was to say many times, "What a great way to learn!" Once, toward the end of Expansion, someone called and asked to talk with Jill. After hearing about our adventure, the woman and her husband began considering it for their family. We could hear Jill's end of the conversation; her enthusiasm and direct positive analysis were so impressive. We commented, "She should be a PR person for home-based schooling."

As part of Expansion we frequently read aloud, and at other times, Jim was busy with art projects, play, inventions, and learning how to use his Dad's tools. He and his Granddad made a waterbed for his room. In the last year of home-based schooling Jim engineered and created his own skateboard, but for the first years he continued to be completely uninterested in the academics. Without his consciously realizing it, Jim learned math by watching me cook and Bill work in the shop, but he had no interest in reading. We were committed to wait for his rhythm of readiness to indicate that the time for him was right. We waited and waited and waited. We kept smiling and trusting. In the meantime, the sparkle had come back into his eyes, and he regained his sense of humor and enjoyment of life. It worked; our reason for adopting a different family lifestyle had accomplished what we'd hoped it would—Jim's emotional core was healing.

When he was nine, Jim was ready to learn to read. His life had developed to the point where he felt he was missing something he wanted. The first thing that triggered his interest was that he wanted to know what the billboards on the side of the highway said, but "by the time I get your attention or Jill's attention, we've gone by." The time had come to learn to read! Without working hard at it, he was up to grade level and beyond in about six months—with no stress, tears, or resistance. Being slow to be *ready* to learn, according to the cultural expectations does not in any way suggest that a child is slow to learn. In fact, waiting until Jim was ready considerably shortened his learning time and increased his joy of learning. He became excited about the new world of reading and gratefully discovered the wealth of books in our neighborhood library. Later Jim started collecting books.

Jim enjoyed the freedom from regimen and the flexibility we practiced. Learning spontaneously was fun and he thought it was so sensible. Practicing reading and math principles only until he understood them, rather than doing a prescribed number of problems, also seemed sensible to him. Later when he returned to school, this common practice shocked him, "Why should I have to do fifty problems, when I get the principle after eight?"

During the flexible, casual, and spontaneous school years at home, Jim recaptured his zest for life and innate eagerness to learn and try new things. He said many times while he was in high school, "I'm so sick of school, and I had five years off. I feel so sorry for the kids who have had no time off." Jim is now a successful young engineer and small business owner, already having achievements behind him that are ahead of the cultural time line. Waiting for his rhythm of readiness paid off for him.

READINESS AND BEING NORMAL

The greatest challenge to parents who are attempting to honor and respect a child's rhythm of readiness is the pressure from society to have children do certain normally expected things at each age. Children starting school at age five is normal, but there are many children who are not ready for that kind of experience at five. There are also many children who may be ready, but would benefit by starting later. Enrolling children in soccer and Little League as early as age five is also normal. Studies show, however, that children can't even envision the field when they are that young, they cannot fully understand the rules until about age nine, and are not emotionally prepared until at least age twelve to handle losing or goofing up in a game without trauma.

A few years ago a neighbor mother was fuming because the coach of her little son's soccer team had decreed that practice would begin every Sunday morning at 7:30 a.m. She told us that all the parents were furious. When we gently suggested that if all the parents, one by one, would just tell the coach they were withdrawing their child from the team, they could be sure there would be no 7:30 a.m. Sunday practices. She acted as if we were crazy to suggest withdrawing from a soccer team. As we left her, we wondered: "Who's in charge of these families—the parents or the coaches?"

"Everyone puts their kids in soccer. It's good for them," we were told on more than one occasion. Unfortunately, following the normal cultural pattern becomes the dominating consideration when families are making plans, choices, and decisions. The attitude usually is, "Well, after all, everyone I know does it that way. How could everyone be wrong?" But these parents don't think to ask the child, so the same cultural mistakes are made over and over. Sometimes parents do ask the children, but in a way that the children know it is in their best interest to answer according to Mom's or Dad's wishes.

The whole family benefits when parenting is based on truly examining what is really right for each *individual* child according to her or his personal timeline and the nourishment needs of her or his emotional core. When parents respond to the readiness of each child, the child is strengthened and the solidarity of the family structure is strengthened as well. The maxim, "No chain is stronger than the weakest link" applies to the family. Giving attention to building the inherent strength of each child, and parent, is certainly worth the time and effort.

READINESS AND THE ADULT PERSPECTIVE

We know so well from personal experience that it's difficult for adults to truly understand their children. We've made erroneous assumptions at times, and we've heard other parents make all sorts of declarations about their children without consulting them. Once when we were visiting a family whose son was taking piano lessons, his mother declared, "Bobby would love to play his newest piece for you." Bobby's sour expression obviously told us that he didn't want to do that at all.

Often parents are eager for their children to be interested in a certain activity in which they, the parents, are interested—perhaps swimming or a team sport. The child's attitude, expressed in body language is saying, "No, it's not time for that yet," or "I'm not interested now," but the parents miss the signal. Experiences that seem harmless, or even fun, to adults, like walking down railroad tracks, can be very traumatic for a little child, and if the child is forced to make that walk before she or he is ready, there can be injury to the emotional core. *If only the condition of the emotional core could be as visible as the condition of the child's arm or leg!*

READINESS AND ASKING

Figuratively, we learned to ask our children to guide us, as the conductor guides an orchestra, in *supporting* them through their developmental stages according to their personal rhythm. We weren't tempted to compare our children's progress to the progress of other children—so unfair to the individuality of each child. Sometimes we asked outright, "Do you want horseback riding lessons?"; and sometimes by observing, for instance, watching to find out when Jim was ready to dress himself. We knew the answer when he started pulling on his socks and putting on his shirt.

READINESS AND THE FREEDOM TO BE

Toward the end of our fourth year of home-based schooling, we explained to Jill that the time had come for her to go to high school because the teaching credential only covered kindergarten through eighth grade. Jill was disappointed that Expansion was coming to an end because she enjoyed the freedom of learning spontaneously and using her own interests as a base for vocabulary building, developing writing skills, and doing research. She appreciated the freedom we had to travel when we wished and the freedom she had to stay in her pajamas until noon if she wanted.

In fact, there was an option. We knew she could stay home for another year and then start high school. When we explained this option to Jill, she enthusiastically said, "Wow, that's great!"

The Rhythm of Readiness

Jill was already prepared academically to enter high school, so we asked, "What would you like to do with your year?" She was like a kid in a candy store trying to decide among all of the tempting candies. She finally chose her treats: "I'd like to spend a lot more time on the organ and learn to sew. Those are the main items. But I also want to write stories, read, play at our vacation house, continue the creative dancing with Mary, Alexa, and Melissa, and do whatever else comes up that sounds good."

The extra year was a delight for Jill. She accelerated her organ lessons and discovered a passion for Bach. We all came to know and love Bach's "Toccata and Fugue in D Minor," which stood out in the extensive repertoire of classical pieces she was learning and enjoying. A friend of ours showed Jill the sewing basics and some craft work, and she began regular sewing classes for specialties, such as sewing with knitted fabric. Jill became the star of the class, and during one of those sessions the teacher asked Jill if she'd like to work for her in her sewing business. On a flexible basis Jill spent a few hours a week basting and doing other basic sewing while watching the woman work. This way Jill learned even more about sewing. Later in high school she created all her own clothes, including her own square dancing dresses. She also had a sideline of making Christmas ornaments. During that extra year at home she and her friends continued the modern dance group they had begun a few years before. The girls created and gave wonderful shows for their families.

Jill was ready and enthusiastic about going to high school the following September, having enjoyed herself thoroughly during her bonus year of childhood. She was often surprised how easily she could handle challenges that "freaked the other kids out." One afternoon she came home from school and described a P.E. assignment the teacher had given the class—to plan and perform a solo dance for the group. Jill loved the idea and had such fun with the performance. But she looked around and saw that some of the girls were in trauma. Nervousness, crying, and extreme fear made dancing impossible for some girls. Jill realized that, for her, the extra year off had made the difference. She moved through the rest of high school with exuberance and confidence.

When we later shared with a friend that we'd offered Jill an extra year of childhood, the friend's reply was, "Of course, you stipulated that she could do anything she wants as long as it's constructive."

"No, we didn't add that restriction," we replied. "The year is supposed to be a bonus year *for her.* How could we possibly judge accurately what being constructive would mean to Jill. She can lie in the sun every day if she wishes."

It is a cliché to describe Jill's joy in choosing how she wanted to spend her year as "a kid in a candy store," but it portrays perfectly the ecstasy she experienced. Many parents would bristle at the idea of allowing a child to truly and completely enjoy herself for a year. Is that responsible parenting? We think it is. This kind of honor of the child and flexibility within principle is one way to put the *joy* into living with children.

To this day, Jill remembers the wonderful time she had socially and the ease of the academics program she experienced, having gone into high school well-prepared and completely rested. She sailed through college and into adulthood with the same confidence and poise.

There was another advantage for Jill that she didn't realize at the time. Her year off coincided with her puberty development. During that time of intense physical change, she did not engage in demanding academic programs and there were no pressures of performance thrust on her as there would have been had she been in school. Instead, she did what she initiated and what she enjoyed. This freed her consciousness to fully support the dramatic physical changes taking place in her body. We believe that the successful, assured, capable, and happy adult Jill has become was in part due to that year off at a crucial time in her development.

READINESS AND ACCEPTANCE

We realize so well that there is little support in our culture to honor a child's rhythm of readiness, because we and our children experienced the lack of it from friends and neighbors during the home-based schooling years. Even though Jill and Jim were popular with their friends at other times—the doorbell always rang after school—for the first two weeks of a new school year they were completely ignored. Jill and Jim suddenly had the plague. The first year, being ignored was a shock. We all pondered, "What is going on?" Finally we figured out that their friends' summer was over and they had to go back to school, but Jill and Jim didn't have to go. The friends were jealous and handled that negative feeling by pretending Jill and Jim didn't exist. The pattern repeated every year, and Jill and Jim never took it personally—they just waited it out. Sure enough, after about two weeks, the doorbell again started ringing.

READINESS AND ROOTS

As you follow your children's lead through the orchestral composition, "The Rhythm of Readiness," you may observe that they are behind in some areas compared to other children in the community. That certainly was Jim's case before *he* wanted to learn to read. Rejoice about this! Your children may live to be centenarians, so what is the hurry? You can be sure they are growing deeper and firmer roots than they would if they were being pushed to stay even with, or pull ahead of, the norm. With strong, deep roots, their emotional core is in good shape to see them through life's challenges without stress and with poise. These children navigate the journey of life with an important edge because they are freer and therefore, happier.

If you choose to use this principle, *the rhythm of readiness,* we urge you not to falter under peer pressure. No one can judge the rhythm of readiness for your children. However, you can become aware of their readiness by observing *them* conduct the rhythm of their lives.

You will find that living joyfully with your children is up to you to implement—the culture can't and won't do it for you. The principle of *the rhythm of readiness,* however, can help you implement the element of joy in your family life. We're grateful that we discovered this principle in time to honor our children according to *their* rhythm. Following their rhythm led our family to a dimension of joy we wouldn't have wanted to miss.

14.

TAKING CARE
OF MOM

THE AIRPLANE TAXIS DOWN THE RUNWAY for take-off and the voice of the stewardess fills the cabin. As she describes the various safety features of the aircraft, she says, "Should there be a loss of cabin pressure, an oxygen mask will appear in front of you . . . If you are traveling with a child, put on your mask first and then assist the child."

This safety instruction is a perfect example of an application of the principle of Enlightened Self-interest: *If the adult has taken care of her or his needs so as to be functioning well, that adult is in a position to be effective on behalf of the child.* We discovered in our family, that when we took time, energy, and money to have our own fun, nourishment, and space, the household atmosphere was lighter and more joyous.

We all understand that in order to function well a person must have a proper balance of food, physical and mental rest, and exercise. Yet on a daily basis, mothers get the cultural message that in order to be good mothers they should be continually self-sacrificing. When the self is sacrificed, there is no self to be optimally effective. Every mother knows the dragged-out feeling, just barely making it from one task or demand to another. Some mothers wouldn't feel normal if they weren't dragging and feeling constantly pushed. A state of pressured exhaustion, however, is counterproductive to the goal of a positive, joyful experience in family life.

Mothers are also pulled down by the intrusion of guilt, which is almost synonymous with motherhood in our culture. Mothers can

Taking Care of Mom

translate guilt into myriad forms, "I'm not cooking enough," "The house is never as clean as it should be," "I spend too much money to keep the household running well," "I didn't get enough done today," "The kids were cranky today; Jason got a C in spelling; I'm a terrible mother." This attitude, which is based on fear, has deep cultural roots spanning back for centuries and affects every mother today. Donna shared with us during a telephone call, "It's an odd day. I don't feel guilty for a change. But I'm beginning to feel guilty because I don't feel guilty." Moms who take time to take care of *themselves* are especially susceptible to a sense of guilt.

Fearlessly take strong and positive steps toward breaking cultural patterns concerning the roles, responsibilities, and value of Mom in order to establish a joyful atmosphere in your home. This atmosphere of joy will naturally include an assumption that taking care of Mom is high on the list of priorities. Then, in *that* atmosphere, the family life together is much more likely to be healthy, happy, and harmonious.

How many budgets include a category for nourishment and growth for Mom and the marriage? Unfortunately, not many. But in fact, that's like expecting to fix dinner without buying any groceries. Just as you make out a grocery list, get into the habit each month of planning activities and intervals of nourishment and growth for Mom and the marriage. Some ideas from other families for taking care of Mom are: a sitter comes one afternoon or one day a week, Dad takes the kids out on Saturday, Mom and Dad have a date once a week and a weekend away every few months, Mom doesn't cook dinner once a week, relatives or friends keep the children overnight.

One of our friends, who is a single mom, shared this with us: "When my children were younger, I always neglected taking care of myself. All the income I made went to the children and their needs. Later, when I began to budget money for my own needs, they seemed to feel more secure and their respect for me and for themselves grew. The children's quality of life rose as mine did." Practicing Enlightened Self-interest benefits everyone.

> **Win:** *During the years we had school at home, the family had breakfast, sent Dad off to work, and then I figuratively put a "Do Not Disturb" sign on my door for an hour or so. The children*

could do as they pleased, but could not disturb me unless the house caught fire. I used my hour to read, write in my journal, sleep, sit quietly with a cup of tea, do a little sketching, lounge in the sun— whatever was the most fun and nourishing for me. I enjoyed a nice renewing time. This gave all of us space and worked very well because, if I weren't rested and nourished, the children would be negatively affected.

You may throw up your hands and wail, "There's no time, energy, or money left over for taking care of Mom." But Moms who practice Enlightened Self-interest find that in catching the vision and shifting priorities, some former necessities that gobbled up time, energy, and money are really not so necessary. The first step is to boldly catch the vision that Mom must have time for rest and renewal in order for the entire family to function well. The next step is for you and your family to shift priorities to bring this vision to reality.

Make taking care of Mom a *necessity,* and therefore, a high priority in your family's plans. This shift creates the all-important key family element, a rested, refreshed, and effective Mom. The family joy naturally follows.

15.

A Secret of Successful Parenting

C HARLES SCHULZ, THE CARTOONIST who created the Peanuts comic strip, says the success of his strip "comes not from adoring children, but identifying with them." The same criterion for success applies to parenting as well. Why is it so difficult to identify with children? We were all there once! Perhaps there are many reasons to forget how childhood feels. One reason for the difficulty may be the heavy burden associated with the responsibility of parenting. Fear keeps some parents locked into concentration on the responsibility, robbing them of the freedom to enter the children's world and stand in their small shoes to look around from that point of view. Another problem that prevents identifying with children can be a busy, overbooked schedule that causes preoccupation with worry or activities unrelated to the children. The attention simply isn't there.

Most parents identify only with the adult world and, unfortunately, believe their responsibility as parents is to mold their children into conformity with that world. Therefore, they don't even try to understand what is going on for the child. A child, of course, has not reached the stage where she or he can function in conformity with the adult world, therefore, expecting a child to do so is like insisting that a fish function just fine in air. We know any such attempt will result in the quick demise of the fish. Anyone who would try to convert a fish to living in a waterless world and expect that fish to survive is not identifying with the fish. But we can learn to identify with, and provide the requirements of, a fish without being one. The principle is simple and obvious in the case of fish in contrast to humans. In the case of parents in contrast to children, however, it appears to be a secret. So few people who interact with children seem to know and practice this principle: *Identify with your children.*

Another obstacle to being able to identify with children is the difficulty of setting aside personal bias and needs, emotional baggage, expectations, and adult assumptions. All this must be done in order to tune in on a *child's* feelings and expectations and to figure out what is best for the *child's* emotional core, consciousness, and personal sense of joy and value.

The failure of parents to become free of fear, personal emotional baggage, and assumptions usually results in their making demands on children that are premature, unreasonable, thoughtless, misplaced, and even extreme. For example, "You'd better get an A on that English test today," is the type of comment that reflects parents' own fears that *their* child will not do well. Parents' fears drive their interactions with their children, making it impossible at that moment to relate to a child's point of view or situation.

A common parenting error is to judge that an activity will be easy for a child because it seems so easy to an adult. This creates a blind spot, which also makes it impossible to understand what is going on for the child.

Marlene was excited when her daughter, Sandra, came home from school and told her that all the fifth grade classes were having a spelling bee. Participation was optional, but the reward for participating was extra credit toward an English grade. Marlene remembered the annual spelling bee as a big event that she anticipated with pleasure when she, herself, was in fifth grade. It had been fun; it was a game.

Marlene made the immediate assumption that, of course, Sandra would participate. "That extra credit will be great," Marlene smiled. She called the teacher and asked her how she could help Sandra prepare for the event and made arrangements to stop by the school the next day to pick up the spelling bee word lists. As the weeks went by, she was so proud of the way Sandra was learning the words, and was sure that if her daughter didn't win, she would be close.

On the day of the spelling bee, the entire family went to the school to watch Sandra perform. Marlene could see Sandra was very nervous and never smiled. She did very well, and then the fatal word came. Sandra missed it. Her face turned white as she made her way to a seat in the audience. She kept looking over at her mother with a devastated expression that seemed to be questioning, "Do you still love me?"

As the family went to the car after the spelling bee, Sandra kept sobbing, "I'm so sorry, Mom. I'm so sorry. I tried so hard. I knew how to spell that word. I don't know what happened. I just couldn't get the letters straight in my head."

Marlene was astonished that Sandra was so upset. She kept saying, "It doesn't matter, Sandra, I know you tried hard, and you did your best. We're proud of you for doing so well." The whole family chimed in, but Sandra was inconsolable.

Marlene began to wonder if she had made a mistake. She looked back to the day Sandra came home with the news of the spelling bee, and realized she never thought to ask Sandra how *she* felt about it or what *she* wanted to do. She had to admit Sandra was never enthusiastic about it during the weeks of preparation and even remembered one time that she thought, with hindsight, Sandra may have been trying to tell her she didn't want to participate. But Marlene had paid no attention and didn't give Sandra a chance to speak, let alone share her feelings. It was clear now that Sandra tried in innumerable ways to skip the drilling sessions, and obviously would have liked to be elsewhere. Marlene wondered, "Why did I, an intelligent, conscientious mother, let this happen to Sandra?"

Marlene was overwhelmed with guilt. Of course, she'd had no intention of putting Sandra through an experience that would be so unpleasant for her and obviously bruise, if not injure, her emotional core.

Marlene had just assumed that because she, herself, had enjoyed spelling bees, Sandra would. Marlene recognized now that the extra credit wasn't really important. She also recognized that if she'd really considered it from Sandra's point of view, she would have remembered that Sandra was somewhat shy among her peers, not completely comfortable at school as she, herself, had been. Sandra was also prone to demand excessive perfection of herself. All of these factors created a terrible combination of personal traits for a spelling bee participant. Marlene clearly had not identified with Sandra, and she had let her own enthusiasm blind her to Sandra's particular personality and preferences.

In the ensuing weeks Marlene and her husband made a special effort to show Sandra how valuable they knew she was. They also tried to help her realize *for herself* her tremendous value as a person, just because she was Sandra. At the same time they were hoping that the needless bruises on her emotional core were healing. Because of her parents' loving care, healing was taking place.

When parents do not identify with a child, that child can feel like a fish out of water. But with effort and attention adults can learn to identify with their children. The results give the children an environment in which they can function without stress and with joy, not only now, but throughout childhood and adolescence. What a difference this solid and supportive foundation can make as adolescents enter adulthood. They are free of fear, failure, and uncertainty.

This principle of *identifying with your children* applies to all stages and circumstances of parenting. Let's take the example of sharing toys. Small children (and sometimes not so small children) have difficulty separating who they are from the things that have become familiar and dear to them. In the case of toys, there isn't much difference in a small child's emotional analysis of "my arm," "myself," and "my toy." Therefore, when children see a beloved and familiar toy in the hands of another child, they feel a loss of stability. The degree of that loss and the degree of reaction to that loss is related to the condition of the child's emotional core and the level of emotional maturity.

If the level of emotional maturity required by a situation is beyond the capability of the child at the time, even having an emotional core in good shape isn't enough to overcome the lack of maturity. To insist that a toy be shared when the child isn't ready is unreasonable, *even though it may be socially correct.* In fact, such an experience can be very frightening to the child. We found through the years of our parenting that a choice often had to be made: "Is my child more important to me than what people will think of me?" If we parents can answer, "Yes," many unfortunate decisions affecting the children will be avoided.

Sharing toys is no longer much of an issue when children reach their childhood middle years and adolescence, but sharing their time often becomes a big issue. It is common for parents to allow and even encourage their children in these age groups to fill their lives with so many activities and commitments with family and friends that virtually every waking hour is shared with someone else or, in the case of homework, assigned by someone else. Parents assume that because the children seem so grown-up now, they are capable of handling their busy lives just fine, as parents do themselves. In fact, a schedule with very little alone time can be very disturbing and stressful for a child of any age. You can help prevent stress-related problems (for example, the development of poor vision) by helping your child avoid time-sharing overload and encouraging the child, instead, to save plenty of free time for herself or himself.

A Native American adage goes something like this: "Never criticize another until you have walked in his moccasins for a day." In other words, "Parents, constantly identify with your child." This doesn't mean corrections should not be made—they often must be. Parents can still understand and acknowledge the child's point of view, however. For example, "I know you are angry that you can't go over to your friend's house today, but you cannot kick the cat." Relating only to an adult point of view, a parent might respond to the same situation angrily, "Don't you dare kick the cat!" Most parents have learned that responding to a child's anger with anger seldom helps the situation or the child.

CHECK YOUR WISE PARENTS METER

Wise parents:

❖ identify with circumstances from the child's point of view at the moment, and govern their words, attitudes, and actions in a way that protects and nourishes the child's emotional core,

❖ make corrections gently and help the child save face in difficult situations,

❖ are alert that their child not feel rejected or worthless,

❖ realize each child is magnificent as a person, regardless of any mistakes that have been made,

❖ won't expect a child to function at a level of emotional maturity she or he has not yet attained or assume that physical or mental capability automatically means emotional readiness.

A Secret of Successful Parenting

These approaches to parenting are only possible if you can genuinely identify with your child. The key to being able to do that is to refrain from having *your own* personal agenda that must be fulfilled through your child. Apply this principle of identifying with your children to all areas of your parenting, and you will have a treasured secret.

16.

FAMILY
FREEDOM

Bill: *When our son, Jim, was approaching driving age, I explained to him that if young men don't value themselves highly, they try to compensate by acting strong and powerful. As part of this act, they often ride loud, powerful sounding motorcycles and make tires screech as they accelerate the cars they drive. Since Jim had not yet reached this stage, we both knew we were not talking about him, but about what he might observe his peers doing in a year or two. "I never thought about the connection between driving styles and the urge to seem strong and powerful," Jim mused, "but now the connection seems so obvious."*

AS JIM AND HIS PEERS BEGAN TO DRIVE, I referred back to our earlier conversation by asking if some of his friends put on the strong and powerful act. He smiled, and said, "Yes, they do." We were two men with an inside joke.

Jim caught the point about driving styles, and he applied it further to also explain why some of his peers put on other acts to appear more manly. As a result, he was not unduly attracted to that scene, and instead, found friends who valued themselves and had no need to put on the macho-manly act. Jim made use of the information he received in advance to keep himself free from needing to act like a macho man.

Win and I had developed a passion for freedom during our early years of marriage. I was an officer in the Navy then, and we endured long months of separation when my ship was engaged in overseas operations. We appreciated the sacrifice that Navy personnel and their families were making in giving up much of their own freedom to protect and insure freedom for the rest of our citizens.

As we became a family, we had a strong desire to honor *family* freedom. We valued the spirit of freedom, and we knew that freedom is the foundation for a joyful family atmosphere. We realized that the freedom of each family member is important because the role each member has to play becomes a dynamic part of the whole family. A high priority for us was to preserve each family member's freedom so that person's role contributed, not only to the quality of life for that person, but to the quality of family living.

When children become adolescents and teenagers, their individual freedom is more severely challenged than in earlier childhood. Whether or not these challenges from the culture are successfully met, determines and sometimes changes, the atmosphere for the entire family. Children lose individual freedom when they unthinkingly adopt the attitudes and beliefs of their peers rather than forming their own attitudes and beliefs. Their peers, in turn, may have unthinkingly adopted the fears and false beliefs of the culture, all of which inhibit individual freedom.

How could we, as conscientious parents, realize our vision of family freedom and joy? We were faced with a dilemma: we wanted our children to be accepted by their peers and be in the mainstream of their world outside our home; we also wanted our home atmosphere to be much more joyful and nourishing than was typical in our culture. As we contemplated this dilemma, we realized that the preservation of our children's joy of individual freedom lay in their being able to listen to their peers and appear to be in the mainstream, yet to be so sufficiently detached that they could successfully stay free of the beliefs and influences which did not belong in their lives or in our family. If we could help our children preserve their freedom, they would have satisfying lives and would preserve the family freedom, which would in turn further benefit the children.

What could we provide that would enable our children to be detached and discriminating? We devised a strategy to give the children advance knowledge of what to expect from their peers and how to interpret it objectively. With this advance knowledge, they could be discriminating and far less likely to adopt beliefs and attitudes that would have been negative for themselves and our family. We followed the strategy with each child from the age of about six through the high school years. This was the strategy that worked so well helping Jim stay free from the need to put on a manly act by driving cars loudly and fast.

In our family discussions designed to provide the children with advance knowledge, we attempted to cover subjects involving cultural beliefs which, if adopted by the children, had the potential of significant negative infringement on our family freedom. We also discussed positive subjects, such as the principle of freedom, that would benefit the children as they moved forward into their independent lives. Both Jill and Jim still respect and honor the principle of freedom for themselves and our country. For example, they are two of the twenty-five percent of Americans who vote; they wouldn't miss it.

In addition to young men's driving styles, other subjects we discussed included democracy, politics, sex, religious beliefs, drugs, drinking and smoking, television and movies, four-letter words, education, athletics, relationships, and personal finance. Our discussions took place in a casual setting as four people having a conversation together, with insights flowing among all of us. The children felt honored and trusted that we were giving them advance information that their friends had not yet learned, or information that their friends might not receive at all.

There was some uncertainty in our minds as we used the advance information strategy. We didn't know of anyone else who had done it. We didn't know if our children would appreciate our pioneering efforts to better their lives by introducing concepts and principles that were different from those the culture offered. But we had looked around at many other families and realized most parents certainly didn't have any magic answers to give us. We could always say, "At least we did try."

The family freedom that we achieved was based on the premise that each family member would act responsibly to maintain her or his own individual freedom and to honor the freedom of the other family members. We held family council meetings in which we often emphasized that along with freedom comes responsibility. We discussed the activities—every family knows them: mowing the lawn, putting out the trash, cleaning the house—necessary to keep the household functioning harmoniously. We defined these activities as some of the responsibilities necessary to maintain freedom in the family. We couldn't be very free if the lawn was never mowed, the trash never put out, or the house never cleaned. *Family* freedom meant all family members participated and all family members benefited. After the chores were identified as responsibilities, we asked for a volunteer to take care of each responsibility. Instead of assigning chores, we honored volunteering, which supported the principle of family freedom.

Of course, there were some family council meetings in which the children didn't volunteer for as many responsibilities as we would have liked, but we felt it was important to honor their freedom to volunteer by not assigning chores. In subsequent meetings we revisited the subject and eventually we had quite an equitable sharing of responsibility.

> **Bill:** *Freedom was a topic of importance to the whole family. When Jill was about ten, I interviewed her and recorded the session. At her college graduation party we played part of that interview which included this story:*

"Jill, if you could be any kind of animal for a day, what would you choose to be?"

After thinking about the question a moment she answered, "Well, I would want to be a bird."

"Why would you choose to be a bird?"

"Because a bird is free, and I always want to be free."

The family and friends at her party clapped in appreciation when they heard this, because they knew Jill had retained her vision of individual freedom.

Why give so much attention to family freedom? A family atmosphere of freedom nurtures the experience of living joyfully. Focus on freedom in the daily living of your family, and help your children maintain their individual freedom from the controlling concepts in the culture. Then watch your children carry into their own adult lives this heritage of freedom.

17.

GUILTY AS CHARGED!

Judge: You have been found guilty.

Defendant: Of what have I been accused?

Judge: You are accused of being an imperfect mother.

Defendant: But, Judge, I've been trying so hard.

Judge: That makes no difference. You are sentenced to feel guilty for the rest of your life.

Defendant: But, Judge, my children won't be with me the rest of my life.

Judge: That doesn't change anything. You shall feel guilty the rest of your life.

Defendant: Oh, Judge! That is a terrible sentence. Is there any possibility of pardon?

Judge: Hmmmm. Well, there is one possibility. Have you always done the best you could do at each moment?

Defendant: Oh, yes, Judge! I have always done so. And I continually strive to make my best better.

Judge: (with bang of the gavel) You are pardoned.

THIS LITTLE FANTASY DRAMA focuses on the feeling of guilt that is common with mothers. In our culture this guilt is so pervasive that few people even realize it exists. Yet among mothers, *especially* mothers who are at-home moms, guilt is a debilitating fear.

Guilty as Charged!

Self-guilt is part of our cultural heritage. For thousands of years, the principal religions of western civilization have promoted the idea that all mortals are guilty sinners. The heritage of guilt continues into the current culture not only in the religious sense, but also as a nearly automatic response to the errors we occasionally make while trying to live as responsible adults. Women receive further suggestions of guilt from our culture because Eve was blamed in the Adam and Eve story and because women were considered inferior to men in the patriarchal heritage of our society.

Guilt is so pervasive that we can easily accept it, even when doing so is not justified. Carrying guilt results in draining emotional energy and losing efficiency, good humor, and the ability to be clear.

Consider the case of a mother who has been pushed to the limit. Dinner guests will be arriving in five minutes and she is tired, nearly overwhelmed with all of the demands of the moment, and facing even greater demands in the hours ahead. She is a person of integrity who sincerely wishes to fulfill her role of parenting well. One of her children picks up the Cheerios box, which wasn't closed, and Cheerios spill over the floor like a new carpet. She yells at the child, but—horrors—she doesn't believe in yelling at her children. Now she has two problems: Cheerios all over the floor and the pain of feeling guilty for having yelled.

Some may say, "But she knew better. She *should* feel guilty. She deserves to feel bad." Yes, she did slip into a pattern of behavior that she abhors, but is there a need to suffer the pain of guilt? She did not deliberately choose at that moment to violate her principles. If she *could* have gotten through that moment without yelling, she would have.

All of us, children included, find ourselves acting badly sometimes even though we know better. We are disappointed and dismayed when we backslide and act in anger, but we don't need to punish ourselves with the pain of guilt. We do, however, need to strive to become wiser, to restructure circumstances and change conditions so that each day our best becomes better. We should not condemn ourselves for making mistakes at a certain moment, but rather we should strive to make the next moment better.

When you go to bed at night, check with yourself: "Did I do the best I could at each moment today?" We'd be willing to guess that *if you're honest with yourself,* your answer is "Yes." As you nod off to sleep, let the thought come, "I did my best today. That's all I can ask of myself. Tomorrow, next year, five years from now, my best will be better."

The principle here is this: At any given moment everyone does the best she or he can, given the many circumstances involved *in that moment.* Resist the temptation to feel guilty when it is not justified. Guilt *usually* isn't justified. Be grateful, instead, for the opportunity tomorrow brings to make your best better.

A person is more susceptible to feeling guilty if she or he does not feel valuable. Mothers are extremely valuable, but unfortunately, they are not generally respected as such in our culture. As a mom, become more consciously aware of your great value, and then you'll find that sometimes being imperfect at motherhood really is not that important. This will help ease the temptation to feel guilty when you don't meet all the challenges of parenting perfectly, and, therefore, you can contribute time and emotional energy to more productive causes. What can be more productive than having a joyful day with your family!

18.

Don't Plant
Those Weeds!

ALKING DOWN THE PARENT PATH often seems like playing
hopscotch through a plethora of traps. Sometimes we don't
even see them, we just find ourselves caught. One of the
traps that is well worth trying to avoid is the rebellion trap, that is,
planting weed seeds of rebellious attitudes and behavior in a child's
consciousness.

Whether we realize it or not, every parent (including ourselves)
has set in motion experiences for her or his child that could cause
that child to rebel in some way. This generally happens as a by-prod-
uct of some action that seems o.k., positive, or even necessary, but is
not positive in a *bigger* picture view. Matt had spent hours setting up
a model train that he'd purchased with his Christmas money. He went
into the study to ask Dad to come and look at his creation. Dad came,
glanced at it, and said, "That's fine, Matt, but you should really have
the tunnel over here, and you have the bridge in the wrong place. It
will work better if you rearrange the track to make a curve over here
and put the bridge there. Let me know when you've finished and I'll
check it." A weed seed has just been planted.

Weed seeds of rebellion can begin to germinate and sprout at any
time, but are most likely to do so as a child becomes a teenager. It may
seem far-fetched, but many weed seeds are planted even when children
are very small. Developing *awareness* and learning to *pay attention* in
order to avoid falling into rebellion traps can reap great rewards.

Don't Plant Those Weeds!

Some of the common rebellion traps are listed below. If you've fallen into a trap, climb out and develop new ways to handle situations. Don't feel guilty—that's a waste of time. You did your best back then with the awareness you had. Just strive to make your best today better than it was yesterday.

Planting Weed Seeds of Rebellion

✦ Never seem satisfied with achievements. "You should do better; it's not enough."

✦ Let your children's time be filled with so many activities, people, and playmates that there is little or no time to just *be*.

✦ Let the entire family get into such a busy pace that there is no opportunity for leisurely, joyful family times.

✦ Push your children into performances and competitive activities.

✦ Give your children no opportunity to feel in control of any part of their lives.

✦ Thwart your children's opportunities to create or think using their own resources.

✦ Allow the stress level in the household to exist at a high and unrelenting level.

✦ Ask the older siblings to be responsible for the younger children and give them authority over the younger ones. (Both older and younger may rebel.)

✦ Assume that one of Mom's primary purposes is to ensure the children are constantly entertained.

✦ Fail to closely monitor the content of programs your children view on television. (Many images children absorb from television and movies create an agitated state in which a rebellious attitude can develop and thrive.)

✦ Fail to convey to your children that you really value them as individuals, not for what they achieve, but for who they *are*.

✦ Let food and eating become an issue for a power struggle.

✦ Carelessly allow the emotional core to be wounded. (Emotional core wounds become fertile ground in which weed seeds of rebellion can grow.)

✦ Overwhelm your children with material things as a substitute for your presence in their lives.

✦ Fail to respect or honor the intrinsic dignity of your children. (For instance, if you demand "Please" and "Thank you" from your children, be sure that you use those phrases when you talk to them.)

✦ Push your children out of infancy, toddlerhood, and childhood before they are ready to gracefully walk on. Capability is not necessarily readiness.

✦ Insist that your children take part in extra-curricular activities in which they have little or no interest.

✦ Carelessly allow your children to be unnecessarily exposed to fearful situations, imaginary or real, including news of tragic current events. (Fear can very quickly and easily escalate into rebellion.)

✦ Fail to take time out to play with your children, doing whatever would be fun *for them*. (One mother in our parenting seminars told us her girls often tried to persuade her to play their "silly" games with them. She wouldn't consider it—she'd be bored to death. She completely missed the point.)

✦ Fail to acknowledge and appreciate effort, even if it fails.

✦ Force learning before your children are interested or ready.

✦ Let the only time you spend with your children be taken up with directing, correcting, lecturing, checking homework, and taking care of physical needs.

✦ Refuse to honor a child's request, "Leave me alone."

✦ Give your children the impression that you do not think they have anything valuable to say by neglecting to create time to seriously solicit and listen to their opinions and observations.

✦ Create family *rules* just for your convenience and rigidly enforce them, rather than establishing *principles* for the whole family to live by.

THE BALANCING ACT

It is not easy to balance your way through the maze of rebellion traps. Are there general guidelines to help avoid planting weed seeds of rebellion? Yes, there are. The first is to understand something about rebellion.

To rebel literally means "to fight against." Rebellion traps are situations created by parents or other caregivers that set up in a child's consciousness the potential for fighting against perceived injustices and unreasonable demands. These perceptions are often absorbed intellectually, but may also be absorbed emotionally, especially in babies and small children. Sometimes resistance is generated and expressed instantly, other times resistance is quietly buried in consciousness and forgotten, only to erupt when greater autonomy furnishes the opportunity to "fight against."

THE CONTROL ISSUE

One common expression of rebellion is grasping for control. There is something in the human spirit that assumes that control over one's own life is an inalienable right. When that right of control is thwarted, there is automatic resistance. Children rebel when they believe they have no control over their lives.

Who or what is, or should be, in control of the various aspects of your child's life? As a parent, you want to exercise principled control at propitious times *with the greatest of diplomacy*. At the same time, you know you must gradually transfer your parental control to your child as she or he matures. It's all a balancing act, and not always an easy one.

> *Bill: Don called, "I'm really afraid that we're losing control of John, and that makes us feel out of control. How can we be kind, but still exercise the limits that John needs at his age, such as, curfews and chores?"*

"Balance the limits with definite areas of freedom that John can recognize and appreciate," I offered. "In a conference with him delineate both sides of the equation—freedoms and limits. Many families write up a contract with clauses that make this delineation very clear. The parents and the child sign, 'I agree to the awarding of these freedoms.' 'I agree to these limits.' The contract lessens the emotional impact and eliminates suppositions and conjectures."

"But we feel John already has lots of freedom." Don replied.

I explained, "That word *feel* is an important one. You feel you are giving John plenty of freedom, so he shouldn't complain. However, most preteens and teens *feel* their lives are completely controlled. Maybe the limits and the freedoms in John's life are equitable now, but if John doesn't see and feel that way, he will continue to try to wrest control of his life from you. This attempt on John's part is causing your discomfort and fear that you are losing control of John. Unfortunately, parents usually dispense controls freely but fail to dispense freedoms to balance the controls. Keeping both freedoms and limits fairly even in the children's minds would help them feel the situation is equitable."

Some of Don's fear involved the parental anxiety about possible unpleasant consequences of giving children too much control of their lives too soon. This fear generates a strong tendency to relinquish control reluctantly and too slowly, which can plant the weed seeds of rebellion. If parents, however, weigh the risks of relinquishing control too soon compared with doing so too late, they will realize the two kinds of risks are decidedly different.

It is easy to know if you are relinquishing control too soon. Try allowing your child to control homework, how much time to spend each week on the Internet, and when to go to bed. You can observe in just a few weeks if any of the decisions to relinquish control aren't working and you can, if necessary, kindly take over again.

It is not so easy to know if you are relinquishing control too late. Since the cause and effect link is stretched so long over time, the consequences of relinquishing control too late may be impossible to correct. We may not even notice until rebellion is in full swing—perhaps years after the rebellion trap was set by being too slow to relinquish control. We can only react; it is far too late to prevent.

Without warning, a child suddenly becomes uncommunicative or inexplicably belligerent and uncooperative. Behavior patterns are markedly changed and decidedly unacceptable. Susie refuses to come to the table for dinner, calls her parents stupid, and slams her door. Her parents react with amazement, "Where did that come from? Who is this? Where did my child go? What do I do now?" During our active parenting days, we felt that the wisest and safest approach was to take more risks relinquishing control early; this, we reasoned, would minimize the risk of long-term problems caused by relinquishing control too late.

We constantly looked for ways and optimum times to gradually transfer control of their lives to Jill and Jim. When they were still quite young, we decided to try transferring the control of their bedtime to them. They were thrilled when we told them they could go to bed at any time they wished, but they had to go to school at the proper time. Of course, there were risks in doing this. The children may have become too tired and gotten a cold or they may have done terribly in school, but if problems had begun to develop, we could have quickly canceled the privilege. As it turned out, there were no problems, and those risks to family harmony were more than compensated by the reward of the children feeling in control of an important part of their lives.

Don't Plant Those Weeds!

For the first three weeks of the experiment, Jill and Jim stayed up far later than we did and were obviously sleepy and tired during the day. Gradually they began to go to bed earlier and earlier. Eventually the bedtime they chose was nearly the same as the one we had previously insisted upon, but now they were in control. It was a win-win situation because it was also nice for us to be free from having to nag them to get to bed.

We used two criteria to determine when we could transfer control to Jill or Jim. Is it safe? Is it likely that she or he can handle the responsibility that is connected with the freedom? Using these guidelines, we often felt confident to relinquish control at earlier ages than cultural expectations.

When a transfer of control is successful, as it was in the case of our relinquishing control over bedtime, the child feels she or he has been given a gift—a gift of freedom, honor, and trust. Each stage of childhood provides parents new opportunities to gradually put a child in control of some part of her or his life.

Every effort you make to become aware of possible rebellion traps in your family is an excellent investment of your time. As you examine the conditions in your personal life that may affect your interaction with your children, as well as the conditions in the children's lives that may cause them to react undesirably, you learn to avoid rebellion traps. As you succeed in not planting those weeds, you will find a new element of joy in living with your children, now and especially in the future.

19.

EDUCATE, DON'T PROGRAM YOUR CHILDREN

To program: to feed into a machine information to elicit a desired response

To educate: to lead out ('e' is an abbreviation for 'ex-' meaning 'out'; 'duc' means 'lead')

HOW MANY HAVE EVER LOOKED at a newborn baby and seriously wondered if its heart knows how to beat, if its throat will swallow, if the stomach will digest, if the intestines will eliminate, if the cells will multiply to manifest growth? We know these faculties come with the child. The child's consciousness knows when and how to take care of these needs. The number of heart beats, the rate of cell growth, etc., do not have to be programmed into the child. Our only obligation to the newborn is to provide nourishment and rest so that these functions may take place.

Does it not logically follow that the child's consciousness also comes with all other needs anticipated within it—when to give up diapers, when to learn multiplication tables, when to go to bed, when to study, and when to rest? And again, our only obligation is to provide the opportunities for these needs to be expressed and met within the individual.

Educate, Don't Program Your Children

A rare and precious seed is planted carefully in a rich soil, watered and placed in the light it wants, fertilized according to its needs, then is *left alone*. There is no need to program the seed to shoot up the stem at a certain time, to produce leaves, buds, and blossoms at prescribed intervals. There is no anxiety as to whether a leaf is produced two inches above the soil or three, or at exactly which hour the bud bursts into full bloom. The plant is allowed to come forth to fulfill itself according to that which is within itself. There are no determining factors imposed from without. The results are a living thing of beauty that enhances its environment as it fulfills its own potential.

On the other hand, consider the common method of training a dog. Its mind and responses are programmed to elicit certain actions and responses: to heel and eliminate outdoors (for our convenience), to beg or dance on two feet (for our entertainment), to bark when strangers come (for our protection). The results are a well-programmed creature, contributing to its environment in a limited and reactive sense.

Programming

One might say that programming is the pouring in of prescribed conformations imposed from without the individual; education is the tender leading out of the glorious potential that is inherent within the individual—each individual.

Dare to EDUCATE your children!

Educating

20.

THE IMPRESSIONABLE YEARS

HOW CAN I PREPARE MY CHILDREN during the *impressionable* years to better meet life's challenges, present and future?" Impressions absorbed during childhood can last a lifetime and, therefore, can affect children's entire lives. Positive, uplifting impressions are, of course, an asset. We have a young friend who was so impressed by an opera singer's performance that his life career was determined. After many years of devotion, he is a successful and very happy singer. Negative impressions can also be an influence. The news often tells us of crimes motivated by impressions absorbed from television. A key question becomes: "Which impressions do I want, and which impressions do I not want, my children to absorb in order for them to progress through life with emotional strength, wisdom, and joy?"

There are two schools of parental thought that address this question. The first school advocates exposing children to all sorts of negativity so the children will get toughened up to endure fear, stress, and hard knocks, and, therefore, be prepared for the "real world." Some examples include exposing children to:

- current events that can be emotionally upsetting,
- problems that are unrelated to them,
- sorrows they have no need to know about,
- fear-inducing suggestions (common even in family movies, television programs, and some children's books),

- experiences that generate fear, and
- abnormal life situations children can't possibly understand.

We were astonished during the Persian Gulf War to learn that the 24-hour television coverage of that event was being watched by families with children of all ages for hours at a time. It was a big topic in school, even in kindergarten, because the children were so hyped up about it. Make-believe war in Saturday morning cartoons—characters bopping each other on the heads—and violence in standard shows on television and in movies is bad enough, but to carelessly expose children to real war was unthinkable to us. Children couldn't possibly understand the war, but they couldn't help picking up *impressions* of danger, fear, and actual tragedy as they watched the television coverage. Did young children have a need to know about the Gulf War?

Adults can reason, and they have a wide scope of experience with which to deal with negative impressions. While adults may have disturbing problems from impressions they have taken into mind and consciousness, and even have bad dreams, this generally is not as harmful for adults as for children who can't reason away fear; they just have to endure it. The school of thought that advocates exposing children to fear in order to be toughened up is not seeing the full picture of what is happening to the invisible emotional and mental structure of the children during that supposed toughening up process.

The second viewpoint, or school of thought, advocates protecting children from emotionally disturbing impressions, so the children will not experience *any* avoidable fear and stress. The emotional core, therefore, will remain intact without fear and with joy. Parents and caregivers who embrace this second point of view will, in addition to protecting, spend time and energy preparing children for the challenges of the "real world" by helping them build a strong physical, emotional, mental, and spiritual base from which to operate in life. The principle is *protect children from negative impressions and expose them to positive ones.*

Establishing freedom from negative impressions for their children means that parents free *themselves* of cultural suggestions that would trick them into allowing exposure inconsistent with their true wishes for their children. For example, the parents of Becky and Kevin joined the neighborhood parents in taking all the children to a children's movie even though it contained frightening elements. These parents were tricked into the cultural suggestion that any movie advertised for children is o.k. for children. They were just not thinking about the emotional core and the effect on it of frightening impressions.

Impressions can be nebulous, undefinable, and elusive. Many impressions are not like a picture of a dog or a statement like, "It is raining." Impressions are subtle, and they can slip into a mind, an emotional core, or a consciousness without any conscious awareness or recognition. Avoiding the type of content that *may* include negative impressions is an excellent policy for adults and children alike.

Parents who are *consciously* well-informed and aware of activities that could contain negative impressions for children can act wisely to protect them from those impressions and provide opportunities for positive ones. Movies, television, and books are, of course, commonly recognized sources of impressions. Parents must also be alert to new impressions in the culture. For example, in the last few years some television commercials and programs have taken a new insidious twist. They are presented in quick scenes that flash at a rate that is actually disturbing to the mind and consciousness. This technique is done to attract and hold attention, which it generally does. Children can be hypnotized and disturbed by the agitated style very quickly. (Of course, adults can be hypnotized as well.) Wise parents avoid exposing their children to this disturbing broadcasting technique.

Judging from what is popular in the movies and on television, it's the in-thing, or even fun, these days to be scared and to fill one's mind and consciousness with gross and grotesque impressions. Commonly absorbed into the mind are the tragedies and the sorrows of the world (real or imagined), the evil, the bizarre, and the negative. These impressions make a tremendous impact and do affect daily living.

Win: I can attest to the fact that impressions in childhood can last a lifetime. When I was about six, a family friend became ill. I heard my parents discuss the lady's illness. I heard the term brain tumor and was very aware of the predicted death that eventually ensued. Through the rest of my childhood I was terrorized every

*time I had a headache. I was sure I was going to die. The condi-
tioned response lasted far into adulthood, but thankfully, it gradually dissipated. Now I am free because I came to the realization
that the conditioning really had nothing to do with my true Self.
If my parents had known how that woman's illness would affect
me, they would have protected me from those negative impressions.
I didn't need to know.*

Protecting children from avoidable experiences of fear and stress
is wise, because exposure and absorption of negative impressions
weakens children emotionally, mentally, and often physically, forcing
them into a state of vulnerability to a multitude of consequences.
Toughening up with negative exposure does not build strength. It creates weakness, instead. The policy of protection provides an environment where strength can build and consciousness can be clear. In this
environment, children aren't constantly battered emotionally, but
instead, are nourished lovingly so they can gain strength to handle
uncertainty well and can have space in their lives to experience joy.
These children develop confidence in who they are and in the value
of their own resources. Instead of feeling victimized or weakened,
they learn to manage their lives by principle and with strength.

There is another issue that subtly influences some parents to fail
to be careful about negative impressions their children receive. The
expectation of suffering is prevalent in our culture. For most people,
suffering is presumed to be unavoidable, and many people actually
feel guilty if their lives are going well. For these people there is no
motivation to make an effort to protect their children from negative
impressions. One mother declared of her son, "He's going to have to
be afraid, disappointed, and confused sometime. He may as well start
now." To her, suffering was inevitable, and the earlier he had to contend with suffering, the better it would be for him in the long-term.
Wrong and wrong. Suffering is not inevitable, and the longer children
are protected, the better prepared the emotional core will be to support them when challenging situations occur. The children will meet
the challenges from a position of strength, rather than weakness.

We found that we could not trust impressions that seem normal
in the culture because the cultural norm is often negative. Practicing

family principles that, in effect, formed a shield around our children, like an invisible positive force field, worked well for us. We kept applying the principles to guide us in choosing what Jill and Jim were seeing, hearing, reading, and experiencing so as to attempt to avoid negative impressions. As the children matured they developed respect for their minds and consciousness and carried their own positive force field with them. Because we protected them throughout the impressionable years, they were clearer, freer, and better able to handle with equanimity negative impressions that later came to their attention. The strength of their emotional core and consciousness was in place to serve them in maintaining their freedom.

Throughout our children's childhood years we practiced the principle, *protect children from negative impressions and expose them to positive ones.* We recommend this principle to all families. The second part of the principle, *expose children to positive ones,* is where the fun for the whole family lies. Looking for and experiencing beauty, harmony, and aesthetics in books, home environment, clothes, nature, and music present so many enjoyable and nourishing possibilities. Wholesome comedy, books, and movies, museums, trips, picnics, and adventures that are exciting and enriching would all yield positive impressions. Opportunities to be creative and develop their talents and interests open the world of the children's own resources to them; they can enjoy the positive impressions they, themselves, produce. Interesting, upbeat, loving, and joyful people are bursting with positive impressions the children (and adults) can enjoy.

When you say, based on your family principles for nourishing and uplifting choices of impressions, "Let's watch this program, not that one," or "Here is a good book you may want to read," you give your children a wonderful gift for life. Even if they don't read the book, they are absorbing the concept of *selection based on principle.*

21.

THE IDEAL HEAD START

WHEN JILL AND JIM WERE VERY SMALL, we enjoyed observing them as they played or slept so contentedly and happily, but then we couldn't help comparing their happiness and contentment with the turbulent, unhappy lives of most of the adults around us. We wanted better than that for our children. We knew, however, that their chances of remaining content and happy as they grew up were slim unless we practiced parenting differently than was normal in the culture. We asked ourselves, "How can we make life smoother and more joyfully satisfying for our children? Can we give them a valuable legacy to carry into adulthood?" The answer that came into mind was to give them an ideal head start.

What did an *ideal* head start mean? What did we need to do?

Bill: The materialistic mania had already begun in the middle class at that time, and we felt that pressure. The men, who were usually the breadwinners then, were judged by how much money they were bringing home. Many of my colleagues were moonlighting with second jobs or had businesses, like owning and maintaining rental houses. In some cases, the second job literally filled all free time.

One day at work Rick told me that he had received a good raise, so he and his wife had bought a bigger and better house in a more

affluent neighborhood. The pattern among a great majority of my colleagues became: get a raise, buy a bigger house. Perhaps this was the
era people began using the term *house poor.*

Win and I made the conscious decision that I would not do anything for financial gain in addition to my professional work, and that
we would not buy a new house as my salary rose. This decision, in
itself, was giving the children a valuable head start in life. We bought
a small vacation home among the redwoods in the Santa Cruz
Mountains. The family spent most weekends there playing together—
creating elaborate Hot Wheel race courses, listening to music, relax-
ing in the hammock on the sun-drenched deck, and exploring the
mountains around us and the beaches nearby.

We enjoyed reading aloud, exploring and discussing principles
and big ideas that interested the children, nourishing a spiritual life,
modeling clay creations, painting and drawing, and collecting (by
finding, not picking) as many varieties of mushrooms as we could
find. We also took many trips together all over the west coast,
Hawaii, and Europe. We were not a hurried family and were careful
not to have an intensive schedule. During those years we had so
many experiences that were intriguing and fun for all of us.

We also decided to ignore the cultural pressure to teach Jill or Jim
academics early. Of course, whatever they learned by their own initia-
tive and interest we supported. We knew they were intelligent.

We trusted that when the time came for academic learning in
earnest, learning would go quickly and the children would do well,
a supposition which proved to be correct.

In contrast to academic learning, we wanted to help Jill and Jim
build a strong base of appreciation for imagination, innovation, and
invention. This base of creativity would form the context in which
they would use *future* academic learning as a support for their adult
goals. We wanted them to have minds that were not crystallized into
patterns and responses that could be limiting. In adulthood the imagination, innovation, and invention did become, for Jim, entrepreneur-
ship and, for Jill, a hobby of designing houses.

We focused on nourishing Jill and Jim's wholeness, intrinsic
strength, and emotional reserve to enable them to move gracefully
into adulthood. Some of the elements of wholeness we considered

important were that the children felt honored, valued, and respected as individuals by us and others, were confident and free of fear, able to participate with ease in social situations, and were thoughtful of others. We wanted them to be equipped with good manners, integrity, and ethics; to have the confidence to be independent of peer pressures; to be mature enough to seek resources of wisdom; and to look forward to life cheerfully.

We could not buy a curriculum for the ideal head start we wanted for our children. We lived it, however, by providing ways for Jill and Jim to experience their own wholeness, which also provided ways for us to experience ours. We look back on those years with so many beautiful memories, joy, and gratitude that we had the privilege to live with these special young people for a few years before they moved gracefully into adulthood.

Desiring to give children a head start is a fine motivation, but the way it is done in our culture today is not always wise and in the best long-term interests of the children. In fact, what parents are led by the culture to believe will be a head start is often actually the opposite, especially as far as the entire scope of their future lives is concerned.

> **Win:** *Several years ago I sometimes had occasion to visit an acquaintance in a nearby neighborhood. Nearly every time I visited, the mother was drilling her preschool daughter on reading and math. It was obvious the little girl had no interest, wanted to be off playing, and furthermore, was just learning by rote what her mother wanted her to know. Little Jacqueline didn't seem to have any understanding of how the various elements fit into the whole process or how the whole process fit into life. When I diplomatically asked about the activity, the mother replied in a tense voice, "We have to do it; her cousins know all of these things already, and besides that, we want her to be ahead of the other children her age." I wanted to ask, Why? but of course, I said nothing more.*

The next year the mother insisted her daughter skip kindergarten and go directly into first grade, even though she had just turned five. Before long the teacher suggested that the correct placement was kindergarten because Jacqueline wasn't emotionally ready for first grade. The mother was furious. She proudly pointed out that Jacqueline could read many words and could add and subtract up to ten. The mother truly thought that because she had given her daughter a head start in reading and math she would be admired, and Jacqueline would be encouraged to attend first grade at the age of five. She enrolled Jacqueline in a private school that placed her in first grade. Then there were new problems. Jacqueline distracted the other children by talking with them and wandering around the room at inappropriate times. She disrupted the class because of her emotional immaturity, not because she was being deliberately mischievous. This is a perfect case of a head start going awry.

What is a parent to do? The cultural pressure on parents to push their children into academic achievement at an early age is intense. Therefore, many well-meaning parents, like Jacqueline's mother, engage their children in this type of activity before they can even understand the math and language concepts or have a personal need or desire to know. This cultural pressure is motivated by the belief that the earlier children begin academics, the better they will be able to understand math and language skills as they progress through the learning years.

But let's look at some statistics: Children in Denmark begin school at age eight, and there is almost no illiteracy in that country. By contrast, children in France are expected to start learning to read in earnest at age five, and the country is reported to have a thirty percent rate of learning disabilities. Our son didn't feel the need or the desire to know how to read until age nine. In six months, without working hard, he learned to read at a level that the average student in school is expected to reach in five years. The added bonus for Jim was that he was managing his own learning. Waiting was more efficient, productive, and rewarding. Forced academic accomplishments can set up learning and emotional problems in the future that are counterproductive to the long-term welfare of the children and make life *more* difficult rather than easier.

THE CHILDHOOD GROWTH CYCLE

Understanding the long-term cycle of childhood growth gave us important insight in providing our children an ideal head start.

The Ideal Head Start

The years from birth to seven or eight, depending on the personal timeline of the child, are physically intensive. This first growth phase ends with the development and eruption of the permanent teeth, which is the last big physical push of this period of development.

The next phase of the growth cycle is the middle childhood years between the completion of the permanent set of teeth and the intensive physical changes of puberty. The body continues to grow but more gradually and less dramatically than in the earlier phase.

Then come the adolescent years when physical changes are again dramatic, and there are dramatic emotional changes as well. The child's body is becoming transformed into an adult body. This completes the cycle of childhood growth.

THE IDEAL HEAD START DURING THE FIRST YEARS

From birth to getting permanent teeth there is much going on in a child's little body. The complex transformation of the infant's body to the child's body is tremendous, and a lot of invisible support in consciousness is required in order for that transformation to go smoothly.

Children develop and learn best during the growth cycle's first phase by moving about. We like to see Deanna and Ryan engaged in activities like playing at a park, running cars around the house, manipulating clay, jumping on the trampoline, exploring new discoveries, building train track layouts, or giving the baby doll in the buggy a long walk around the house or garden. Deanna and Ryan naturally intersperse their movement and exploring activities with short times of sitting or lying quietly while listening to music or a story, or doing nothing. Although they don't *consciously* do it, this variety is important for punctuating movement activities with rest. Movement and rest is the natural pattern for these early years. When children have to sit at a desk or when they sit in front of a television set or a computer, *except for a short time,* this pattern of natural development is not honored.

Restricting movement and teaching reading during the first physically intensive phase of the childhood growth cycle can result in negative consequences, rather than the positive ones parents expect. Many people believe there is no connection between the body and the

mind or between the body and mental/intellectual activities; they see
no reason to wait until after the physically intensive years to introduce
and encourage academics. Neurologists tell us, however, that important brain and eye muscle developments that support learning to track
a line of words across a page don't take place until age seven or eight.
Therefore, forcing reading before then can cause stress and eye problems. Trying to learn to read while the physical and emotional developments are still in progress that support being able to read is like
trying to drive a car while it's still being assembled.

> **Bill:** *We're not saying that a child who learns to read at four will
> not be successful in the business world. Of course, that child can
> be successful, however, possibly at a physical and emotional price.
> I have known many successful, talented men in the business world
> whose personal lives are not happy ones. Perhaps the reasons are
> related to their becoming adults before all of the purposes of child-
> hood had been fulfilled. Parents, of course, want their children to
> be successful in the entire spectrum of their lives; however, the
> culture does not support a balanced childhood.*

The emphasis on intellectual activity for small children is relent-
less. A salesman talked Cynthia into buying a set of encyclopedias,
stressing that her children of two and three should have these
resources available as they grew, so they would have a proper head
start. Cynthia critically sacrificed to buy this encyclopedia set because
she wanted to be a good mother. By the time the children were ready
to use them, however, the set was out-of-date and not comprehensive
enough for their needs.

Too much, too soon is not better. For example, teaching little
ones about colors, numbers, letters, names of objects, and soccer does
not pave the way for easier learning later, and instead, robs children
of important independent play time. In fact, unnecessary rote learning clutters and fragments any child's mind, emotional core, and consciousness, which in turn, can cause disorientation from the Self.
This makes later *appropriate* learning more difficult, and in many
cases the process of learning is made agonizing, slow, and painful.
Many diagnosed learning disabilities and vision problems are nothing

more than the results of this inappropriate pressure in a child's life. There are more productive ways to give your children a head start.

Our grandson, Ryan, is four now. We have often read to him, and he has figured out the function of written words and is beginning to ask what a word or phrase says. We are careful to give only the information he asks for and to leave him free and clear to progress at his own pace. This method honors his ability to direct his *own* learning, which is part of the ideal head start concept. As long as Ryan is allowed to do that self-direction, learning will be fun for him and will go very quickly and easily at the right time. One of our favorite parenting principles is *supply information when asked and only as much information as asked for.* Turning a one sentence answer into a long lecture is often so tempting.

Protecting children from being bombarded by premature intellectual learning is not easy. When we bought a software program for our grandchildren, we had to look a long time for one that only encouraged play—not academics. For now, we want computer time, as well as all of their time, to simply be fun in an uncomplicated environment.

THE IDEAL HEAD START DURING THE MIDDLE YEARS

The middle childhood years, after the physically intensive years and before the commencement of adolescence, is the time to encourage a child's intellectual and mental capacities to begin their long maturation process. The middle years head start will be ideal *if* the activities are not excessive, competitive, too intense, or coupled with too many extra-curricular activities, *if* the children have a personal need and desire to know, *if* they believe that learning is fun, and especially *if* the children are allowed to learn at their own pace and according to their readiness and interest. The preparation by the ideal head start in the first years has given the children of the middle childhood years a consciousness, mind, and emotional core that have room to accommodate the intellectual adventure of these middle years with ease, enthusiasm, and the joy of learning.

This ideal way of life wasn't happening for the daughter of one of our friends. School was a constant nightmare for Debbie. She always felt overwhelmed, continually criticized by a teacher she considered to be mean, and ridiculed by the in-clique, who teased her about the teacher thinking she was dumb. Needless to say, this stress spilled over to the family life as well. Life had become a trial.

Debbie's parents wisely realized their daughter needed to be rescued, and that would require a lifestyle change. When they offered homeschooling to Debbie, she thought it over carefully, and then gratefully accepted. The sun immediately began to shine in the household again. Debbie quickly realized there was nothing wrong with her intelligence. She just needed a slower pace for awhile, some loving reinforcement, and time to herself. Her parents gave Debbie the space and support that will benefit her for the rest of her life. When she was later ready to go back to school, the new school experience was fine.

Having an ideal head start during the first years and the middle years prepares the children, as well as the whole family, for ideal teen years.

The Ideal Head Start during Adolescence

The early part of adolescence is devoted to puberty, and the later part is intended as a time of adjustment to those dramatic physical and emotional changes. The small child doesn't usually notice the changes taking place which transform his infant body into the body of a child. However, a child experiencing puberty is personally aware and consciously involved physically, mentally, and emotionally in these new changes. The intensive emotional changes and adjustments continue over a period of years, often well into young adulthood, and need ongoing tender loving care, attention, and support. More energy, intrinsic strength, and stamina are demanded of the child's consciousness to keep life running smoothly while experiencing puberty than was required up to that time. Therefore, this is an important time to lighten up on academics, sports, extra-curricular activities—everything that drains strength and stamina. Interestingly, the two periods when children require the most sleep are in the first years and during adolescence.

The ideal head start of the adolescent years provides a resting period during which important personal intrinsic resources can be developed and strengthened. There is also plenty of time to get acquainted with this new body, its new functions, and a whole new set of emotions. During this ideal head start, space in life is also provided for the young people to experience new feelings and perspectives, and to explore into their new worlds, which need to be understood. There is much going on subjectively for the adolescent.

Our culture provides little rest for these precious young people. Instead, stress is accelerated. It is impossible for intense physical/emotional development *and* intense mental/intellectual development to both take place smoothly at the same time. Enlightened parents will figure out a way to take the cultural pressure off their adolescent children, and again, as they did during the ideal head start of the first years, give them space to grow and simply *be*. Any academic efforts should be restful, not stressful. Parents who protect their children from cultural pressure are making a valuable investment in their children's future and in a high quality of family living.

Providing an ideal head start is not as easy during the adolescent years as it was in the first physically intensive years because the cultural pressures are more insistent, but it can be done. Each family must develop its own plan, and the parents, who know these young people best, can best devise a plan that will be fruitful. Start the plan with a list of what you want to accomplish, such as providing plenty of opportunity for your adolescent child to build physical, mental, and emotional reserve ready to be drawn upon when college begins. College can be an intense environment, and young people often arrive at college overwhelmed and nearly exhausted, instead of refreshed and ready to plunge in. Could this be a cause of many of the common college problems?

When you have compiled the list, find the principles to apply that will help accomplish the objectives. For example, the principle of freedom would specifically apply to relieving pressure and stress in certain areas over which you have control. You can achieve this relief by, perhaps, encouraging your child to quit a job and to use the time simply to be lazy, to pursue a hobby, or to do nothing. Doing nothing is doing *something* in this context. Don't complain if your teenagers sleep until noon on Saturday; encourage them to sleep all day. The culture says, "Go, go, go." Enlightened parents will say, "No, no, no."

One of the reasons parents pick up this "Go, go, go" pressure is that they are influenced to fear that their children will not do enough to succeed in life. Success in life comes from providing children a balanced childhood that recognizes their wholeness. Striking a balance means that in addition to preparing academically for college and career, priority must be given to acquiring self-knowledge, building the physical, mental, and emotional reserve for college and life, understanding personal business affairs (the checkbook, for example) and understanding relationships.

Many parents dread the teenage years, feeling helpless to prevent the trauma that is accepted as normal in our culture. Much *can* be done to create an environment in which children are free to develop and grow at the rate which is optimum for them as individuals. The teen years can provide many memories of fun and fulfillment for the teen and the whole family. As you and your children live by principles, you will find family life will be harmonious, efficient, and joyful. All that needs to be done for the children to truly succeed in life will be done without trauma and with confidence.

✧ ✧ ✧

There is an ideal time in your children's growth cycle for each and every development and experience they need in order to have a successful and joyful life. If you pay close attention to all phases of the growth cycle, honor them, and look to your children to direct their own pace of development and learning, you are giving them the Ideal Head Start.

22.

ALL THOSE LESSONS!

Win: As a mother of young children, I found myself caught up in the lesson thing. All my friends who were mothers had their children enrolled in a variety of lessons—music, Hebrew, swimming, etc. All the mothers, including me, kept a schedule and chauffeured the children hither and yon during the week. In our zeal to provide the children with advantages, we weren't even considering the children themselves and what they might want to do. After all, didn't parents know best?

ONE DAY I WAS SITTING QUIETLY, not even thinking about anything in particular, when the thought came to me, "It's too much; it's too much." At that time our children were enrolled in art, swimming, and horseback riding lessons. Because they are three years apart in age, they were in separate swimming classes. That meant lesson trips four days a week.

I pondered the thought, "It's too much," for awhile. What a relief to know I could look at the lesson thing and make a change. I was tired of that routine; it was a chore. I envisioned Jill and Jim being very disappointed if I told them we would be stopping *all* lessons, so I decided to offer them each one lesson series and hoped they would choose the same one.

All Those Lessons!

I reluctantly shared the news with Jill and Jim, which they took very matter-of-factly. Then I asked them to think about it until the next day when we'd talk again. They didn't wait until the next day, but told me in a few hours, "We don't want any lessons at all. We'd rather just be free to do what we want." Wow! I was surprised, but delighted. I'd been putting myself out for them because I thought they wanted the lessons. But the children were just going along with the lessons to please *me*.

It's easy to see why the lesson routine didn't work out: I was doing it for the wrong reasons. All the other mothers I knew were doing the lesson thing. In my naive and inexperienced state, I thought that because everyone else was doing the lesson thing, I should be doing it. After all, I did want to be a good mother. But now I was learning that some of my concepts of a good mother weren't very enlightened.

That was the first time I realized that a good mother tunes in on what really nourishes her individual children, rather than merely following the cultural program and assuming *that* had to be right for them. Asking them what they wanted had never occurred to me—yet it was so simple. Assuming that the cultural filter is right can lead one astray.

Our daughter, Jill, who is now a mother herself, heard about a gymnastics class for children of Ryan's age. Her first thought was: "I wonder if Ryan would like it. I'll only take him if it is fun for him." What a wonderful motivation! She was going to figure out a way to find out if *he* really wanted gymnastics and would enjoy it, and then follow that lead.

How many times have you heard, "The children will do this or that, *because it is good for them*"? What about making it possible for the children to do things just because those things are fun? Studies have shown that forced learning or *being taught* when there is no interest or desire can be stressful, and therefore, counterproductive. Children learn easily and well when they are interested, self-motivated for the right reasons, and having fun.

As a culture, let's rethink *all those lessons!*

23.

EXPECTATIONS

Children should be seen and not heard!

W E ALL SMILE WHEN WE HEAR THAT OLD SAYING, because we know our children today are certainly not being brought up that way. That saying reflected one of the expectations in our culture a century ago. There has always been a long list of what is expected of children in our culture, and the expectations change with each generation. Therefore, the programming of children changes to fit the ideas and social structure of the time.

We see many differences in what was expected when our children were small, compared to present expectations. For example, Jill and Jim were expected to just play and have fun until first grade when the introduction of *beginning* reading and math took place. At that time kindergarten was designed simply to be playtime within a group structure. Legally children were not required to be in school until age eight. Now, in some school districts, children are expected to be prepared to begin learning to read in kindergarten, and must, in California, legally be in public school, or an alternative, by age six.

Expectations

THE CHANGE OF THE FAMILY STRUCTURE

What has changed? Not the children. They still have the same biological, emotional, and intellectual pattern in consciousness. The culture's *expectations* have changed as the elements of the culture shifted.

One of the changes in the culture that has dramatically affected children is the shift in the structure of the typical family. There are more single-parent families than ever before, and a single parent usually works at a full-time job outside the home. Also, there has been a major exodus of Mom from the traditional family as she has gone back to work to add a second pay check to the family coffers. In many households there has been a shift from both spouses having jobs to both spouses pursuing careers. The demands on the parents who have careers are generally more stringent than on those who just have jobs because working long hours, bringing work home, and making business trips are often necessary.

Family dynamics are different from what they were twenty-five or thirty years ago, because children are less of an integral part of parents' lives now. As far as parents' interaction with their children is concerned, much of the parents' attention and energy goes to providing the necessities—baby sitters, tutors, food, clothing, and shelter. There is often no time, energy, or money left to take care of the subtleties of life—the emotional core, the family relationship and fun together, the child's feelings, the atmosphere of joy, and the teaching of good manners, discipline, ethics, and thoughtfulness.

Most families just survive from day to day, and feel lucky to even do that. Recent studies have shown that in a typical American family the members of the family have become so involved with television, outside activities, and for the parents, jobs, that parents spend an average of six minutes per day in meaningful interaction with their children. We know some children who feel that their parents don't spend any meaningful time with them. One little boy told us, "If I could have any toy I want or a Saturday morning with my Dad, I'd choose my Dad."

Many children have come to feel they are a burden or inconvenience for their parents. Eric shared with us, "The whole time I was a kid I felt just like I was a family cat that they had to feed; I didn't get much more attention than that." Parents would be horrified to think that their children feel they are a distant side-line to their parents' lives, but many children do feel that way and never tell their parents.

A close friend of ours, who has worked outside of her home since her children were very small, is just starting up a business in her home. She recently told us that her beautiful daughter, who is already self-sufficient and in her own apartment, was visiting one day and complained, "Mom, you never have any time for me! You are always at that computer, day and night!"

"It dawned on me so clearly," our friend lamented, "that Megan was not only telling me about feelings she has now, but she was telling me about feelings that she has been carrying around for years. I always work! I'm still more involved with my career than with my child."

The shift of expectations has swung toward expecting children to fend for themselves. They are expected to be competent at an early age; indeed, children are sometimes forced into a position of having to act as though they are competent, whether they are or not. Many parents are frazzled and overworked, and they need their children to be competent and not too demanding. Some children rise to the occasion, some do not.

Sue has two children, a teenager and a preteen. Until four years ago she was an at-home mom, but now she must work. Sue and her children were prepared for this change in family lifestyle, in part by Sue's daily practice of principles that she had learned in our parenting study group. In order for the children to fulfill their obligations Sue has taught them how to use the public transit system. Besides where the children must go, they may also go anywhere they choose in the large city in which they live. Sue thoughtfully established guidelines of responsibility for this freedom and keeps track of the children by their pagers. The solution is working because Sue doesn't expect more of the children than they can comfortably manage. They are doing well and are very proud of the fact that they are trusted to be on their own out in the world. Many children in similar situations where they are expected to handle themselves almost like adults don't fare so well, perhaps because their emotional core is not in good shape, they are not mature enough for the new responsibility, or they are not adequately prepared for the new expectations.

CULTURAL EXPECTATIONS

Expectations can weigh heavily upon children. This burden often causes problems that seem to be totally unrelated to the expectations. Pressure to correctly identify colors, get an A, kick the goal in soccer, play perfectly at a recital, win a track race, or take care of themselves for long periods of time, can cause children to feel *they* are not as important to their parents as their accomplishments are. Then when expectations are not met, the children have a fundamental feeling of devastation for having failed, even after doing their best to achieve what they had been led to believe was so important. The children assume, "I'm worthless, no good."

Brian shared with us that this is exactly what happened to him. His Dad often worked in the evenings, so he didn't participate in the family too much. Mom was alcoholic, so Brian had to vacuum, dust, and clean the house if it was going to be cleaned. He bought the groceries, cooked, and took care of the laundry. Then there were his school obligations. He worked hard, well aware that most of the other kids weren't expected to be parent and child at the same time. He longed for some recognition and support, "You've done a great job; we're proud of you." It never came. Instead, he received a constant barrage of criticism.

Brian sadly recalled, "Whatever I did, it seemed to be wrong, not enough, or not the right time or way to do it. My parents always expected more; they were never satisfied. Or sometimes, perhaps worse, they just ignored me as though I wasn't even there." This translated into an adult pattern of automatically being excessively critical of himself, feeling that *whatever* he does is not enough or is not right. Brian is striving to build a new set of expectations for himself based on the many talents and fine attributes that he has, rather than expecting himself to function according to unreasonable demands as was the pattern when he lived with his parents. When he can remember and appreciate what he has to give and realizes that he has fulfilled the reasonable expectations, he is content.

Children do not have the maturity and sophistication to realize that when they fail to fulfill the expected achievements, there are valid reasons, such as an expectation not being consistent with a child's personal timeline. Even though the reasons are valid, children can't apply that logic, so the emotional core—that place from where the automatic reactions to life come—is bruised every time there is a feeling of failure.

A parent's own damaged emotional core is often the source of harsh behavior during interactions with the children; seldom do parents intentionally inflict unreasonable demands on their children. In Brian's case, his parents had unreasonable expectations of him and failed, because of their own neediness, to give him any encouragement or support. In other cases, parents may feel burdened by the weight of parental responsibility, and to lighten their burden they impose unreasonable demands or expectations on their children.

Many parents feel they do not have unreasonable expectations of their children; indeed, *they* may not, but the culture does. Cultural expectations affect children because parents, and also children, pick up expectations from the cultural atmosphere just as if the words were spoken. Sometimes the words *are* spoken to children by parents who have picked up the cultural expectations: "Gail is sleeping in a big bed now; it's time for us to get you a big bed," or "Sarah Jones was selected for the debating team. You, of course, will be selected too, when you take debate next semester!"

Many books detail expectations adults should have for each age group of children, often implying that parents should be concerned if a child's progress differs from these expectations. Every child, however, doesn't fit the cultural timetable. In fact, few children do, but for survival most children learn to conform as best they can—often survival to them means getting that all-important smile from Mommy or Daddy.

Children do not all become ready for *anything* at the same age, yet in our culture there is an insistence on using age as an indicator of expected readiness. If their child does not fulfill this expectation, parents fear something is wrong either with their parenting or with the child. Many parents feel *they* have failed if their children are not performing equal to, or ahead of certain age expectations. Since this feeling of parental failure is so difficult to cope with, children are pushed to conform to cultural expectations so the parents can relax and feel o.k. about themselves.

The fear of being labeled an inadequate parent diverts attention from the true indicators of individual readiness, some of which are physical development, emotional maturity, the condition of the emotional core, and the individual interests of the child. When parents give adequate attention to *these* indicators of readiness, a conflict with the cultural expectations often arises because the cultural expectations indicate otherwise. Then a choice must be made: insist the child conform to the cultural expectation as best she or he can *or* trust and support the indicators that are intrinsic to the child.

EXAMINING THE CULTURE

When we began taking a good look at the expectations of the culture for our children, we could see many expectations are valid, such as good manners. But a closer look revealed that many other expectations were not always in the best interest of our children, for example, the expectation that *all* children should start the school years at age five with kindergarten. We asked ourselves, "How can it be possible that all children are ready for kindergarten at five?" We became convinced of the importance to objectively examine the cultural expectations as well as our own personal conditioning, knowing that our expectations could be a form of control. Then we set about to free our children from negative expectations while preserving the positive ones. In some cases, this yielded choices: Jill did not choose to go to kindergarten; Jim did. There was no negotiation in other cases, however, such as practicing courtesy.

We encountered two major challenges as we tried to be discriminating about cultural expectations. First, we had difficulty objectively determining the validity of cultural concepts about childhood development and cultural expectations of children because we, ourselves, had been raised in the same culture. Second, after determining what we believed to be a more valid set of expectations, we sometimes had to act counter to the culture in order to adopt our preferred choices.

We discovered that attempting to examine the culture we live in is somewhat like a fish attempting to examine the water it lives in. We take the cultural influence so for granted that we think its influence is *our own decision*. Our not understanding our culture as separate from us gives rise to some erroneous thinking and faulty judgment, which often results in fear that our children are not measuring up or that they will be harmed. We call these negative effects the results of not seeing through the *cultural filter* to that which is *true* for us, but, instead getting stuck in it and believing that the cultural expectations are our own expectations. When we got this sorted out, we experienced great freedom.

When we parents can't see through the cultural filter, we don't question the belief that our children should give up breast or bottle or begin writing book reports at certain prescribed ages. We may also accept ideas that suggest the children should be exposed to stressful experiences during childhood to prepare them for adult life stress. The fears of failure that parents accept about a child's progress or well-being also contribute to the cultural filter effect—not seeing clearly.

As we look through and beyond our cultural filter, we honor each child as having her or his own timeline of readiness. We know that a child's being slow, according to the culture, to get *ready* to learn is very different from a child's being unable to do so. Often it's not even being slow, rather it means *that particular child is in exactly the correct place in her or his own timeline.* (Probably most children who seem to be ahead have really just been pushed ahead.)

Much of what we define as culture is a collection of *expectations.* Culture is generally created by, changed by, and perpetuated by adults, yet it profoundly affects the lives of children. As we were raising our own children and were involved with other families, we began to wonder if the many cultural expectations demanded of children supposedly for their benefit might, in fact, be designed more for the benefit of adults, school systems, and even toy companies.

Toy companies are always looking for new markets—a good business practice, but maybe not good for children. The mini-bike for small children is an example. Betty told us, "We bought a mini-bike for Steven. It's just the right size but he can't ride it without the training wheels, and that is not really riding a bike. We took the training wheels off and Steven got so frustrated, he refuses to go near it now."

Bill: I asked, "Can a little child really be expected to understand the principles involved and have the physical coordination and emotional maturity all together to ride a bike well?"

Betty replied, anxiously, "If kids this age couldn't do it, they wouldn't make bikes for this age. Steven is just backward, I'm afraid." The bicycle industry created an expectation. Is the expectation realistic and kind?

No one said parenting is easy. Parenting means mentally being many places at once. There are always many tasks to be done and often challenges to overcome. Parents feel pressured just keeping life sorted out minute-by-minute. The job of sorting out and discarding negative expectations and preserving the positive ones is difficult, not only because of the cultural filter effect, but also because of the intense, close involvement with our children. This kind of involvement often makes seeing the issues clearly almost impossible. When parents do manage to be clear, making their own choices isn't always comfortable because making those choices may mean acting counter to the culture. For example, we didn't take our children to view the scary children's movies. Most other parents did. We made a choice.

A few years ago we attended a soccer game in which children ages five and six were playing. The edges of the field were lined with parents screaming instructions at their children. After a time-out we saw the coach push a tiny boy into the game enthusiastically, but urgently, saying, "Run that direction and kick that ball." The little fellow looked confused and reluctant. He glanced over to the crowd of parents—perhaps looking for a rescue—hesitated, then ran slowly out onto the field.

We sat on the ground next to one of the little girls who had been in the game. We asked her what she was supposed to do out on the field. She responded, "Well, I was supposed to bump the kids with red shirts out of the way and kick the ball that way," pointing down the field. "But I don't like to bump the other kids, and I don't like them to bump me. My Mom told me it's rude to bump kids, and besides, [with a sigh], I never get anywhere near the ball to kick it. I'm no good at this. But my Dad keeps telling me I have to do better." Later, we found out her Dad was one of the parents holding a video camera and screaming at her while she was in the game.

"Are you having fun?" we asked her.

"The coach says we're having fun and that's what my Dad says, too," she replied.

"But are *you* really having fun?" we asked again.

This precious little girl of about six years looked at us with a pained expression on her face and said, "Yes, I guess. We're supposed to."

As we stood at the edge of the field and looked at the kids' tense, screaming parents, we wondered, "Why don't *they* play soccer and leave their kids alone?" Many, we knew, truly thought soccer was good for the kids. They were well-meaning, but painfully wrong, at the expense of their children's well-being. Instead of creating situations for the children in which *every* child felt valued, free, and happy, the parents were creating situations in which their children were knocked around, literally and emotionally, and probably most of them felt confused, worthless, and fragmented. This is the influence of the cultural filter. These particular parents did not personally generate the idea that soccer is good for the kids, but they bought into the idea and perpetuated it.

More than one parent conveyed to us their belief that to be responsible as a parent, their child had to be in soccer. The expectation in the culture was that parents should place their children on a soccer team at the earliest possible age to give them an early start in sports. And of course, Mom or Dad often can't avoid communicating to the child, at least subliminally, the expectation that she or he will be a valuable player on the winning team.

This injustice to our children is happening because parents accept and rationalize the expectations from the culture, believing the culture can't possibly be wrong. But the actual results of this acceptance and rationalization are usually quite opposite from those the parents would say, and truly believe, they want for their children.

Optimally, every child should be able to go to bed every night having had a winning day in whatever was going on in her or his life.
But the culture isn't set up that way.

SETTING OURSELVES AND OUR CHILDREN FREE

Win: *Expectations have power. When I was teaching school, I became aware of an experiment in one of the district's schools in which the children in a particular class were given IQ tests. Before the psychologist gave the results to the teacher and the parents, she reversed the scores: The children who had actually made the*

highest scores were assigned the lowest ones and vice versa.
You can imagine what happened. The children began performing
according to what the teacher and the parents expected of them.
The way the teachers and parents talked and conversed with the
children, assigned tasks, critiqued work, and even their gestures
communicated to the children what was expected. The children
responded according to the expectations.

Performing according to expectations is not unusual. For example, a child's twos can become terrible twos, and the teens can become terrible teens, primarily because they are expected to be. The *expectations* set up attitudes, environments, and reactions that bring about the expected results. In reality, the *expectations* raise our children, not the parents. While this statement is generally true, few parents recognize that the sources of their parenting policies are simply the expectations of the culture. Many parents unquestioningly try to fulfill those expectations, without considering the source.

There is another way to raise a family: Education in the *true* sense of the word. To educate means to *lead out*. Rather than pouring expectations into children, true education is a leading out of the real, individual Self of the child that is waiting to grow and blossom if given a chance. The true Self is always magnificent, whole, beautiful, eager to learn, creative, and joyful.

You can enjoy the magic of your children as you set yourself and your children free of the expectations of what they *should* be doing according to the culture. This freedom releases them to be who they are. Children love this freedom to *be,* and they thrive in this environment where their natural joy of being and learning can be expressed.

24.

THE THRILL OF A MAGNIFICENT MARRIAGE

AN IMPORTANT STEP TOWARD BEING GOOD PARENTS is being good marriage partners. Therefore, paying attention to the marriage nourishes the marriage *and* the children. Parents who show their children a magnificent marriage are giving them a valuable gift.

Do you remember what it was like when you became engaged? The wonder of this special relationship was exhilarating. After the engagement there was the excitement of the wedding, the honeymoon, and being married. Then the excitement began to fade, sometimes imperceptibly, as a Fourth of July sparkler gradually fades and dies. One reason this fading happens is because the emphasis in life shifts. The emphasis before the wedding was on the relationship and getting to the marriage. Once there, many couples literally give no attention to the marriage, expecting it to survive and thrive simply because they are *there*. Of course, expecting the marriage relationship to beautifully grow in spite of giving no attention to it is a fantasy.

It is astonishing to observe how soon after the wedding the priorities in life can shift from fulfilling the potential of a magnificent marriage relationship to other priorities, like money, possessions, hobbies, and careers. These other priorities are fine, but not as a substitute or compensation for the lack of a magnificent marriage.

Another reason the newlywed sparkler begins to fade is that our cultural patterns of relationships emphasize adversarial attitudes and territorialism between people. A couple's courtship and engagement times are filled with efforts to please each other, but as a marriage relationship begins, each partner tends to stake out her or his territorial rights for the long-term. The process of establishing and maintaining a long-term balance between the interests of the two partners easily slips into competition because of the strong influence of competitiveness from our culture. The structures of the sports and business worlds are based primarily on competition. So it is no surprise that after the wedding there is a shift of emphasis toward competition. The battle of the sexes describes a common destructive marriage pattern which is often so subtle that people aren't aware it is happening.

> **Win:** *After the wedding, a couple tends to push aside the marriage; when the children come, the marriage becomes even more remote. A woman called me, upset, angry, and afraid because her husband was spending a lot of time away from home and was having lunch regularly with his secretary. During what became a lengthy conversation, she self-righteously said, "My children come first with me." She was shocked when I told her that perhaps the only reason her husband might be drifting away was because she was giving all of her prime attention to the children.*

In another marriage, the wife left suddenly. The confused and astonished husband told me, "I had no idea anything was wrong." To be completely surprised when a spouse leaves can happen only if a person is not paying attention. Sadly, most married couples give one another and their relationship very little quality attention. It is not uncommon for couples to split up after the youngest child leaves home. The husband and wife find that without their common interest in the child they no longer have a relationship.

Our culture doesn't furnish couples with a handbook of enlightening guidelines for creating, and then living, a magnificent marriage. In a world of mind-boggling new technology, relationships still struggle in the dark ages. The many broken and unhappy homes and mediocre marriages attest to this. But the marriage is the foundation of the family. So the family foundation crumbles when the marriage is neglected, is not working well, and is far from magnificent.

Children have an acute ability to sense the atmosphere and the consciousness—the invisible indicators of how Mom and Dad feel about each other. Some parents believe their marital troubles are not touching the children because the parents never let on in the presence of the children, but the children cannot be fooled. And don't forget, the parents' marriage, for better or for worse, becomes a model for their children's future marriages.

Joan and Mark seemed to be perfect for each other. They were both educated, poised, attractive professionals who had spent the early years of their adulthood developing a refined philosophy of life and learning how to be balanced, confident individuals. Both had grown up in homes where the parents' marriage was troubled and eventually failed. But Joan and Mark were so well-matched, how could they get into trouble?

After the wedding, life together seemed to go smoothly for Joan and Mark as long as there were no challenges to face. But when a challenge did arise, they found that neither one of them had an internalized pattern of a successful marriage upon which they could draw for guidance. Without a pattern they found it very difficult to work as a team and maintain confidence in each other.

Then their first child arrived. Suddenly the partnership skills they had developed by trial and error were not adequate. They were forced into parenting, and they were drawing on the only parenting and family skills they had—the ones they had acquired, from the child's perspective, in their respective childhood homes.

Joan and Mark were astonished to discover how totally unprepared and incapable they felt as they tried to hold their marriage together and be good parents. Having been successful in other significant areas of their lives, they fully expected to manage quite well both marriage and parenting. What they had not realized was that marriage and parenting skills are largely acquired in childhood, and they had missed out.

As a result of a lot of dedication and work, and with the help of mentors, Joan and Mark have kept their marriage together. Even at the darkest times, they never lost their vision of the magnificent possibilities of marriage. What a precious gift it would have been to each of them if their parents had shown them the thrill of a magnificent marriage. This, Joan and Mark are now determined to do for *their* children.

How can a couple facilitate this special relationship—a magnificent marriage? For one thing, make the effort to shift to a balance between children and the marriage by bringing the marriage back into focus. This new balance in life cannot be achieved without consciously spending time, attention, and sometimes money. A date one evening a week and a weekend away every few weeks are two ways to capture this important time.

Another way to create time alone is to carve it out of daily family living. Children will, if allowed, fill every moment of their parents' lives. No child has the maturity to say to her or his parents, "I know you'd like some time alone, so I'll go into my room and play without interrupting you for an hour." However, children can respond positively when a parent says, "Now we are going to have alone time. You may do whatever you wish in your play area, but do not interrupt or disturb us in any way, unless the house catches fire." We found that setting up this temporary limitation on the children served as an effective *do not disturb* sign. Parents will have to judge when the time is right for their particular children; parents with preschool children can usually create short, quiet, alone times of perhaps ten minutes.

Specifying a definite time limit is important. Before children can read the clock, setting a timer works beautifully. Using a kind and loving voice that conveys, "there is no negotiation," is also important. Children can tell if you are wavering and may take advantage of that opening to make it seem impossible for you to have time alone.

Children who have experienced tender loving care of their emotional core and who feel valued and happy will graciously honor the parental request for time alone. Children who have not had a positive childhood experience may feel rejected or fearful until they feel valuable. Time alone is very nourishing for children as well as adults. Therefore, when the parents are having their quiet time, the children can have that treat for themselves. If there are siblings, time to play together with no parents around can be enjoyable.

Making time alone every day, for each spouse and for the couple, is good time management with the built-in reward of nourishment for each individual and for the marriage. If a spouse arriving home from work can warmly greet the family and then slip into the bedroom or study for even fifteen minutes of alone time, there is a considerable improvement in the quality of the evening.

You can use your time alone as a couple to renew and rebuild the marriage. This special time together excludes talking about the kids and watching television. Start by remembering the magic you knew and loved before and immediately after the wedding. Then build your marriage this time, not on the shaky sands of competitiveness and secondary priorities, but on the firm ground of:

- positive priorities and patterns,
- constructive attention to one another and the marriage,
- understanding based on enlightened wisdom,
- genuine appreciation of each other,
- self-confidence that doesn't require a constant defense or the control of others, and
- cooperation in a genuine partnership.

A magnificent marriage is possible by first, believing it is possible, and second, reserving ongoing quality and quantity time to enrich the marriage. You will be thrilled, and so will the children.

25.

SINGLE PARENTS CAN DO IT!

I AM A SINGLE PARENT. Can *I* live joyfully with my children?" Based on our years observing the lives of single parents, the answer is, "Yes." Living joyfully with children yields a nourishing experience for each member of the family. The nourishment helps the members of a single-parent family feel their family is whole and complete even with the absence of one parent from the home.

Single parents who have succeeded in maintaining a joyful family atmosphere have told us they benefited greatly from adopting these guidelines:

- Realize you are an endless resource.
- Create support systems for yourself and your family.
- Honor your children's relationship with the absent parent.
- Show your children you are a balanced person with a full life.
- Include in your family's activities experiences with joyful two-parent families.
- Create a family structure of friends, relatives, and mentors.
- Take care of yourself and be lighthearted.

Each of these guidelines for single parents is, in fact, based on one or more of the principles that support living joyfully with children. The entire set of principles applies to both single- and dual-parent families, but let us focus on the guidelines and related principles that apply especially to the challenges facing the single parent.

The key to realizing that you are an endless resource is to first recognize your true Self. As you recognize the infinite, perfect, and complete nature of your true Self, you realize that you are to your family an endless resource of love, patience, ideas, spontaneity, play, education, giving, and intelligence. You have a built-in ability to parent. You might not be realizing it at the time, but it is all there. You are the best thing that happened to your child, despite the level of your income or the degree of your education. Acknowledge that realization every day and you can't go wrong. You will find yourself discovering just the right book to support you, finding just the right new friend, hearing about a job opportunity, learning how to rearrange your time with your children in ways that work, thinking up special activities that are perfect for you and your children, but most importantly you will be learning to trust your own true Self as a single parent.

There are many possibilities for forming support systems for families. Support systems are especially valuable in freeing a single parent from feeling burdened in having to carry all the parenting responsibility.

Some very useful support systems for the single-parent family involve assistance from other adults, such as caregivers, peers, and mentors. However, no outside assistance is necessary to create the most useful support system—a structure of principles. There are two benefits you, as a single parent, will find when you create a structure of principles to guide your family living. Parenting is much less stressful when you use principles, and the caregivers who assist you can be more supportive of your child if they know and follow your family principles.

You ask, "How can I get the caregivers for my children to honor our family principles?" You may be surprised by the willingness of your caregivers to join with you in implementing for your child your family's principles. As we have shared many of these ideas in our seminars through the years, parents and teachers alike have said, "Of course! It seems so right. I just wish I had known this earlier."

The element of the absent parent is often a concern for a single parent. One of our single friends had this advice for other single parents: "I regret that I allowed bitterness about the shortcomings of my relationship with my daughters' father to affect my girls. They didn't need to know that I felt angry and frustrated with my ex-husband. It wasn't until my daughters were teenagers that I realized as clearly as if I'd seen a big sign along the highway saying, 'Don't you see? When you talk badly about your girls' father, you are hurting *them.*'" Here is where support from friends, mentors, and family comes in. Talk over personal frustrations with other adults who might be able to show you ways to change your situation and old emotional patterns that are ineffective. The freer the children are from negative feelings about the parent who lives out of the home, the more opportunity they have to develop a workable relationship with that parent. This is key to any child's emotional health.

Family wholeness can be built on the recognition of the true Self of each family member, including the parent who lives away from the family home. Helping your children to recognize and honor the Self-value of their absent parent reinforces their own sense of value.

The principle of balance is especially valuable when you are a single parent, because the intense desire to be a good parent in order to make up for the absence of one parent easily slips into building one's entire life around the children. We parents show children how to stay free as individuals by our having a balanced life that includes them but is not wholly concentrated on them, thereby allowing them to develop their own interests. "When I began to take care of my own life," one single mother wrote, "my children had new respect for me. They have always known that I loved them, now they know that I also love myself."

A single mom shared with us, "I think single parents must go through oceans of guilt over how they are parenting. I wanted to be a super parent and attend all the PTA meetings, spend lots of quality time with my children, and somehow manage to pay for ballet lessons and new glasses in the same month, but it didn't always turn out that way. I also yearned to grow as a person: I was interested in dating, I wanted to finish my college degree, and I pined away just to be able to curl up with a good book with no distractions. It was as if I had *three* children all those years—my two children *and* myself, all needing attention. The person called Mom, who was to look after these three just wasn't making the grade most of the time." This description of how a single mom felt as though she herself was being neglected shows the importance of the single parent developing a life balanced by activities independent from the care of the children.

Single parents have a responsibility that pertains to dating, just as married parents have a responsibility to support the marriage. A single parent may or may not choose to date, but in either case there is a responsibility to respect the individual freedom of each child. A dating parent who brings a date into the home will want to use care and consideration not to disturb a child's sense of freedom. The child may feel pressured into social interaction that, for a child, is awkward or uncomfortable. A parent who does not date will want to use equal care to insure that she or he does not become socially dependent on the children, thereby robbing them of their freedom.

"How can I teach my children marriage skills when I am a single parent?" This parent wisely knew the children would not acquire from high school or television the skills needed to be good marriage partners. Children learn about marriage skills gradually as they observe marriages during the childhood years. Therefore, it is important to include in your family's experiences time with couples and two-parent families who demonstrate the skills of a magnificent marriage. As your children become ready for discussions about relationships, you can increase the value of occasional times with skilled marriage partners by reviewing later with your children the partners' patterns of interaction. By thoughtfully and lovingly providing your children opportunities to see magnificent marriages in action, you are giving each child invaluable skills for her or his own magnificent marriage.

We have observed that single parents who live joyfully with their children know and practice the principle that *to live joyfully with others, one must first live joyfully with oneself.* Just because you are a single parent, you are not debilitated or just half there. You are a complete parent just as you are. The sense of worry, fear, or guilt can be dropped, even for only a few minutes a day, to let the joy flow through you and spread to your whole family. The crucial secret of keeping life balanced as a single parent is to keep yourself and your children free from fear. As you lighten up and take care of yourself, you are showing your children and the world, "Yes, single parents can do it!"

26.

YES!

"HEY, DAD," CRIES DAVID, the family eighth grader, as he bursts into the room, "I just finished writing a story. Wanna read it?" "No, not now, Son," replies Dad without looking up from the desk, "I'm paying bills."

"But, Dad, it won't take long," pleads David.

"I said 'No.' Don't bother me now." replies Dad, still not looking up.

Disappointed, David wanders around the house until he finds his mother reading in the family room. "Mom, I just wrote a great story. Wanna read it?"

"I'll come to your room in a few minutes." responds Mom, barely looking up from her magazine.

Mom finally comes into David's room almost a half hour later, and David eagerly hands her his story. She reads the entire story without comment and when she finishes, she says limply, "That's very nice, David, but you misspelled some words. Hand me a pencil, and I'll mark them." After Mom marks the words she adds, "Be sure you get these corrected and learn them. I'll test you tomorrow after school." Then she leaves the room. She also leaves a boy whose spirit is crushed. He feels decidedly rejected and devalued; in his mind his creative story had become part of who he is. David's mother goes back to the family room feeling good about having caught those spelling errors. After all, that's what good mothers do.

To David, his mother had implied, "No, your story isn't important to me; your spelling is," and his Dad had implied, "No, you're not as important to me as paying bills." Both of David's parents were involved in activities they could have easily interrupted in order to immediately respond to David's eager request. Why didn't they?

One possible reason for their responses may be the influence of a subtle, but definite cultural concept of parenting: to be in charge *all of the time* is to be a good parent. David's parents had interpreted being in charge as not allowing David to interrupt them. For David's mother, being in charge all the time also included being in charge of the correctness of his spelling. She could have said, "Yes!" to the moment by reading his story with a big smile and then sharing nourishing, uplifting remarks for his spirit, such as "That's a great story, David. I really like the way you have the elephant talking so amusingly to the lion." She would not have mentioned the misspelled words, although she could have made a mental note to point out the errors at a time completely disconnected from his story writing activity.

Parenting by the compulsive "I'm in charge all the time" process of No takes many forms—insignificant, unreasonable, extreme, or unkind.

For example:

- "No, you may not eat that cookie, eat this one."
- "Don't walk on that side of the sidewalk; walk over here."
- "I'm too busy to play with you now." [Really being driven by], "I can't drop what I'm doing to play with you, then *you* would be in charge, and I wouldn't be in charge all of the time."
- "Put your toy here, not there," even when it really makes little or no difference.
- "Your report card is pretty good, four A's and one B. I want to see that B pulled up to an A on your next report card."
- "If you don't brush your teeth right now, you're getting a spanking."
- "No, your idea is not good. Do it the way I said to do it."
- "I told you to clean your room. Put all of your books on this shelf, not that one."
- "Don't splash *any* water out of the tub."

Yes!

These statements and the resulting children's obedience are all ways of affirming, "I'm in charge all of the time, as parents are supposed to be. Therefore, I'm a good parent and a good person." When statements like these constantly fall like rain on a child, the spirit of that child is crushed. For these parents, to be in charge all of the time has become more important than what is happening to the emotional core of the child. This particular cultural program for parents means that *what* the child does really wouldn't matter. The parent simply feels that in order to be a good parent something wrong must be found, and the child told how to make a correction.

Most parents would not articulate, "I'm making these constant corrections because I must be in charge all of the time." This pattern is usually accepted as helping the child make important improvement in behavior, attitudes, or skills. Helping children improve is reasonable for responsible parents to do. But when this parenting pattern is *actually* coming from "I must be in charge all of the time," parenting becomes the equivalent of a continuous "No," whether the word is verbally used or not. The cultural message to be in charge and to initiate improvement is so subtle that most parents don't realize what they are doing; they would not *intentionally* crush the spirit of their children.

Parents are ultimately in charge, and children need to know this. But if parents are in charge of every moment, children have no room to grow. Their growth—mental, emotional, and spiritual—is stunted. Perhaps this restrictive atmosphere affects the physical growth as well, because what is in the mind and the emotional core does affect the body.

One of the principles that we keep handy is: *Choose your issues carefully.* Applying this principle in parenting will ensure that the kids don't feel jerked about all of the time with "No" and "Don't" in the large variety of forms that these directions and corrections are given.

The many things children do right and well, unfortunately, often elicit no comment or positive gesture. Therefore, "No" becomes almost a constant companion, slowly draining the child of self-confidence, weakening the emotional core, and similarly affecting the ability to function freely, happily, and well. Parenting by the process of Yes! is a better way.

Recently we received a letter from a friend who has been studying with us for several years. Her daughter, who is fourteen, wrote about an important person in her life for English class. Our friend enclosed excerpts from the composition.

> "Janet Morgan is more than just my Mom. She is also my teacher, counselor, religious leader, confidant, and friend. Mom has helped me through difficult times in my life.
> She hardly ever gets fazed when I am in a bad mood. If I feel upset, guilty, or left out, I know I can tell Mom. She always makes me feel like everything will be all right."

Clearly, this Mom has been parenting by the process of Yes!

Win: *During one of the parenting study group sessions I was leading, the difference between parenting by the process of Yes! and parenting by the process of No was discussed. Carla went home and checked her conversations with her children for a day. She was shocked to discover "No" and "Don't" fell out of her mouth countless times, sometimes in a very unpleasant tone of voice. She also discovered that she inferred "No" or "Don't" or "Do that differently" frequently in non-verbal ways. She decided to correct that habit, beginning immediately.*

Carla was upset when she didn't even get through the next half hour. Her little son came out of his room having put his pants on backwards. Without even thinking, she lashed out, "You didn't get your pants on right. Fix them." She'd begun to be sensitive to the No problem, so she could see that he was crushed. He'd been proud of getting his pants on at all. She figuratively stepped back and saw that, for his age, the way his pants were on was completely insignificant. Instead of ignoring the backward pants, which she should have done, she had inflicted unnecessary pain of rejection onto this little child, inadvertently causing a dent in his emotional core. This is the last thing she wanted to do. She had been so caught up in managing his behavior, she'd never noticed what her criticisms had been doing to him. She almost cried as she watched her sweet little boy walking, head down, back to his room.

Yes!

The incident changed Carla's life. At the next study group meeting, she admitted that she was having a difficult time changing a habit that had been long standing and deeply ingrained. She'd been constantly saying, "No" "Don't!" "Change from your ideas to mine!" in many different ways for so long, not only to this younger child, but also to her older children. Although she wouldn't have guessed it, she could now see she had picked up the cultural program: to be in charge all the time is to be a good mother. How she wanted to be a good mother!

Carla accepted a new definition of *good mother.* Instead of endlessly finding fault, she began seeing her children with new understanding. She realized she hadn't been seeing them as individuals, people with rights and feelings who were looking to her for nourishment and supporting love. Now she knew she did not have to be in charge every moment in order to be a good mother. In fact, the way she'd been trying to mold her children into her image of what a good child of a good mother is had been the opposite of being a good mother.

Carla began looking past insignificant clumsiness and unimportant infractions of her little rules and ideas. Instead, she consciously began honoring each child's uniqueness and valuable true Self. She replaced her various No's with Yes! in every way she possibly could. She used body language, words, gestures, actions, and surprises, like placing a wee gift under a pillow, baking favorite cookies, or taking the children, individually or together, out for a special meal. She said in many ways,

Yes, you are a valuable person.
Yes, you are doing well.
Yes, you are a delight to me.
Yes, your opinion counts.
Yes, I like *your* idea.
Yes, I surely do love you.
Yes, you can do anything you want this afternoon.
Yes, it's fine that you're not a perfect miniature adult.
Yes, it's o.k. that your homework isn't perfect.
Yes, you can have control over part of your life.

Carla told the study group that she was having a wonderful time, enjoying herself, the family, and life so much more than she had ever before experienced. Later she realized that in saying Yes! to the children, she was really saying Yes! to herself, and it felt good.

By tipping the scales toward Yes! the occasional really important No's were automatically beginning to be expressed very thoughtfully, kindly, and gently—often without even using the word. For example, "Do you think it would be a good idea to plan some special time just for yourself on Saturday, instead of going to the mall with your friends all day?" She would listen to the child's thoughts about it, and then carry the conversation forward as kindly as possible.

Carla was astonished when she realized there had been an ongoing tension in the house because she'd been programmed to constantly look for behavior, ideas, or achievements to correct, change, and criticize in her children. She wanted, instead, to encourage the development and expression of the individuality and potential of each child. As she practiced Yes! more and more, she saw the level of happiness and joy in the family rise. Peace replaced the constant tension, and behavior problems all but disappeared. Her children, who now felt valued, could drop their own struggles of neediness and defensiveness caused by her constant criticism and directions, and instead, express what they naturally were—cooperative, relaxed, and joyful.

Once Carla realized her *true* purpose as a mother was to provide growing room for the children in an atmosphere of being valued, she had new freedom. She was free from the behavioral pressures that she now understood had been harming the emotional core of her children. What she had thought was so right, had been definitely wrong. Carla shared with the group that she had always felt like some invisible someone was hovering at her shoulder all of the time with a big record book watching to see if she was always in charge of her children. She had the feeling that if she were ever caught not being in charge, she would receive a black mark. What a relief to realize the invisible someone was just the faceless culture, and she could ignore it with impunity!

Carla's experience of turning her parenting from the process of No and Don't to the process of Yes! affected every part of her life. The children were more relaxed, cheerful, and cooperative. She felt better about herself than she ever had, and she was free from worrying about what other people might think of her parenting. All this netted an additional bonus: her marriage was much more joyful for both her husband and herself. Carla found out that we parents *can* live joyfully with our children and doing so spreads joy to the rest of life.

When Carla told the study group that shifting from No to Yes! was one of the most marvelous experiences of her life, everyone celebrated.

27.

WHO ARE YOU?

Win: *Barbara called one Sunday afternoon, discouraged and a little frightened. She explained that her son, Greg, who had just turned seventeen, had also just turned impossible to communicate with. They couldn't talk about anything without his becoming hostile, defensive, and uncooperative. Worse, perhaps, was the fact that she kept becoming upset, angry, and also defensive. She said, "My son seems to have gone away and an impostor from some bad movie is standing in his shoes."*

"Do you look at him and feel like asking,
'Who are *you*?'" I inquired.
"How did you know?" Barbara replied.

I explained that we could empathize. There was a time after Jill and Jim went back into school, following our home-based schooling experience, that they seemed to be wearing masks. Words kept coming out of their mouths that we couldn't recognize. Especially frustrating were their assertions that *we'd* changed: "You feel . . . about me," "You expect me to do . . . ," "You're going to explode because I got a B in English," and on and on. Jill and Jim knew us well and knew we had never reacted as they described. So, who were these people standing in front of us? They couldn't be Jill and Jim even though the bodies looked familiar.

I told Barbara that we had thought a lot about this phenomenon of misidentification that had suddenly come upon the children. I further explained that before this began happening with Jill and Jim, we became aware of cultural influences and what we came to call the *cultural filter*. We had come to realize that many of the beliefs and thoughts we assume are our own, in fact, are merely suggestions present in our culture; the suggestions act as a filter keeping us from seeing clearly what is really true and really right.

The mysterious behavior of Jill and Jim was the result of their picking up suggestions from the culture about Mom and Dad that were not true. They had become stuck in the cultural filter and were temporarily jerking about as marionettes at the end of strings, simply saying and doing as dictated by the puppeteer—the cultural filter. As in all puppet shows, it seemed like the marionettes, masquerading as Jill and Jim, were making the statements, but the statements were not really coming from them. If the children had been free of the marionette strings and operating from their true Selves, they would not have made those remarks to us. As time went on, Jill and Jim cut the strings, and they were free again.

"Exactly what happened to Jill and Jim is what has happened to Greg," I declared. "Greg has picked up, as they did, the messages embedded in the cultural filter, and he is repeating them as if they are his *own* beliefs and thoughts—which they are not. You can be sure other parents have heard exactly the same things from their sons and daughters, so those remarks are not original with Greg. The remarks weren't really coming from Greg, but you became caught in believing he was expressing what *he* thought and believed and, of course, it upset you."

I continued, "The next time you have a conversation with Greg, look just over his head and imagine there are marionette strings attached to him. Remember that typical cultural beliefs and thoughts for a young man of seventeen are pulling those strings and jerking him about like a marionette. Prepare yourself ahead of time to refuse to accept as belonging to Greg the ideas that he has picked up that you know aren't really a part of who your son is. He *can* cut those marionette strings and be free. Whether he will be able to cut them at this particular time of his life is something you'll have to wait and see.

Who Are You?

As you refrain from *reacting* as you have been, you help him feel free to cut the cultural filter strings and return to the Greg you know."

Barbara mused, "I guess I've been a marionette, too. I've been reacting with anger and getting so upset, and I really didn't want to do that to him. I understand the cultural filter now and can cut my own strings. I hope he can cut his."

Barbara and I spent a lot of time on the phone that day discussing ways she could strive to cut her own strings so she would be better able to help Greg cut his strings. The same principle can be applied to any age child and to any relationship. We can be free of repeating cultural filter programs, whether the programs are for boys or girls or Moms or Dads.

About a month later Barbara called back, with immense gratitude, to report that great progress had been made, in spite of the fact that old habits had been hard to break. Understanding is freedom, and Barbara certainly experienced that truth. She'd followed the strategy she and I had worked out and was exhilarated with the freedom she had attained. She knew she was making progress because Greg was shocked that his mother was no longer reacting with anger and getting upset.

Barbara also reported that Greg was feeling much better about life, even though all of his marionette strings were not yet cut. She was pleased to see that Greg was dropping a lot of his defensiveness, although she was sure he didn't consciously realize it. Furthermore, Barbara was applying the same principle of looking for marionette strings in her relationships with her other children, who were younger; she found it worked like magic! Maybe those children won't become marionettes when *they* are seventeen.

28.

NOT IN
OUR HOUSE!

Home Sweet Home! What an apt phrase!

E'VE ALWAYS KNOWN our home is a strong influence on the way we feel and function, so we've paid a lot of attention to establishing home as a special place—a sanctuary. To us a sanctuary implies beauty, peace, harmony, and joy. A sanctuary is not only a physical structure, but also an atmosphere, an atmosphere of nourishment, rest, growth, and enjoyment.

We all want our lives to be worth our time and our children's lives to be worth their time. The atmosphere of our home is an important factor in determining how well we achieve these objectives. Home can be a sanctuary or a place of pandemonium. In spite of good intentions, many people helplessly watch as pandemonium erupts in their home. If nobody is paying attention, the pandemonium may just seem to unexplainably explode and burn like a fire that starts with spontaneous combustion. In an atmosphere of pandemonium thinking clearly is difficult, tempers are short, creativity is usually impossible, anger and frustration can quickly erupt, and control is lost. Home doesn't have to be that way.

Anyone can create home as a sanctuary, but in contrast to the eruption of pandemonium, a sanctuary atmosphere of nourishment, rest, growth, happiness, and fun doesn't just happen. It must be consciously created and then maintained. Making home a sanctuary requires setting new priorities, taking time, spending energy, and encouraging cooperation.

One important key to creating a home that is a sanctuary is to be discriminating about the influences that we *choose* to allow to enter and reside in our home. If a package were delivered to your door, and you saw that it was not addressed to your family, you would refuse it. The delivery person would take the package back, and it would not enter your home. In the same way we would refuse a wrongfully addressed package, we can learn to discriminate when influences inconsistent with our values and standards for living are presented to us.

How do you keep negative influences out of your home? You stand guard at the door of your home, refusing entrance to the unacceptable influences that would intrude if not turned away. Influence, good and bad, is coming at us constantly and invades our homes through the telephone, visitors, television (whenever the TV is on, influence is pouring into your home), movies, the Internet, books, friends, acquaintances, service people, and ideas that family members carry home from the culture. Remember, influence, negative and positive, also comes from sources, represented as authorities, that we would like to trust without question. Acting as a guard at the door means discriminating based on principles and sometimes making choices that are counter to the cultural belief systems.

The word *discriminating* has been used so heavily by social movements to imply something negative that its very important positive meaning has almost been obscured. When you discriminate between the negative and positive influences and declare, "Not in our house!" to the negative ones that would produce a place of pandemonium, you are creating a sanctuary and teaching your children an important skill. Therefore, the process of making and keeping your home a sanctuary accomplishes two purposes. It provides your children with the immediate benefits of living in the sanctuary, and in addition, it provides them life-long tools and skills to be discriminating in *all* parts of their lives—wherever they are and whatever they are doing.

The influences in our culture today include far more intrusive and potentially harmful suggestions to children than have been formerly present in the culture. At the same time families, which are the children's only real defense, have generally become more fragmented and ineffective, except perhaps on a physical and materialistic level. Cultural support for emotional well-being, moral attitudes, ethics, good manners and values, social skills, strength of character, contentment and happiness is not as strongly present for parents today as it was thirty years ago. Now parents must be aware that they can no longer depend on the culture and must promote these values on their own. Therefore, enlightened parenting includes full responsibility for teaching values.

One way enlightened parents can counter the negative influence of the culture is to implement one of the most important principles of parenting: *Just because something is common in the culture does not mean it's o.k.* If any thoughts come to you that are common in the culture, question the quality of that influence.

When our grandson, Ryan, was younger, his Mom picked out a video of Winnie the Pooh because it's normal for children his age to watch gentle Winnie the Pooh. She set the video up for him to watch while she worked in the kitchen. In a few minutes she heard Ryan crying; Rabbit was lost in the forest. Sure enough, Ryan had been frightened by a scene that would have seemed benign for older children.

Now, Ryan's Mom is previewing everything before Ryan sees it, and his younger sister, Deanna, doesn't watch anything yet. Previewing is easy with the convenience of a VCR, and well worth the effort. Although there are some basic principles that would apply to all children all of the time, only a child's parents or frequent caregiver can preview wisely for each child because every child is in a different place. If two children are watching a video or program on television or listening to a story being read, the needs of the younger one must, of course, take precedence.

When we shop in book stores for Deanna and Ryan, we look for beauty and harmony in the presentation. We look for stories that are nourishing, uplifting, and tastefully humorous. In our opinion, some children's books are not suitable for children at all. Many fairy tales are terrifying; some stories are appropriate only for older children. There are books that are delightful except for a few words. If we buy those books, we choose words we consider to be more suitable and paste them over the offending ones or we substitute different words as we read.

Standing guard at the door of your home as far as movies, books, and software are concerned means previewing them so *you* may judge the suitability for your children. The on-going question might be, "Do I want my children to be influenced by this image, idea, concept, attitude, or way of handling life?" What children see and hear can affect their lives and therefore, family life, for years. Previewing is a good investment of time.

A friend told us that she was talking with her neighbor about an animated children's movie she had recently seen. Several children in the theater began crying when the wolves attacked the heroine, Belle. One mother had to take her screaming little boy out of the theater. Our friend ended her description by guessing, "There were lots of sweet little kids having nightmares last night."

The neighbor innocently replied, "But it's normal for children to have nightmares." Yes, it does seem to be normal for children to have nightmares, but it's not o.k. Nightmares create an emotional disturbance that children don't need in consciousness and the family doesn't need in the house. Sometimes nightmares do just happen with no apparent cause, but parents standing guard at the door would never consciously expose their children to any influences that even *might* cause nightmares.

Influence is the business of the advertising professionals. "Buy our product, not theirs." Executives of toy companies begin planning a year and a half before a particular Christmas what toys the children are going to have to have or they will just die. In some homes it seems the toy companies are in charge of the family, not the parents. Beware at Christmas time.

Influences come blatantly, but also come seductively. Even the most conscientious parents can be tricked into condoning or encouraging influences and activities that set up attitudes and patterns that have invisible, negative effects on their children, sometimes long after a particular incident is forgotten. The errors in parents' judgment happen for a variety of reasons. One reason is the difficulty in judging whether or not a particular influence will be a negative one in the near-term or the long-term. We remember that while we were immersed in the throes of day-by-day, hour-by-hour parenting, it was not easy to stop and examine every idea or thought that came into our minds, yet the ideas that came into mind were not always our own thoughts and were, therefore, influences that deserved careful examination. Parents who take the time to examine ideas that seem good at the moment find that many ideas may not be worth the risk of future cost, because acting on them may create problems for the future.

For example, picture a small child becoming upset and beginning to cry because of a painful bump or another child having knocked down the tower of blocks he just built. The mother quickly runs to the refrigerator, grabs a bottle and sticks it into the child's mouth or grabs a cup of milk and encourages him to drink. Ah! Silence!

While much easier on the ears at the moment, providing quick rewards over and over by popping up with something to drink or eat sets up a conditioning in the child's mind: each time something upsetting occurs, comfort and compensation must come through drinking or eating. Milk or juice are the child's drink. With this childhood conditioning, a teenager and adult can quickly turn to some form of alcoholic beverage. The habit of turning, as an adult, to food or drink for emotional comfort, rather than for physical nourishment, often begins in childhood. A better long-term solution for cacophonous crying is ear plugs. Let the child cry while you hold and comfort her or him. Crying, in and of itself, can be an important healing agency. Acknowledge the frustrated hurt feelings with kindness so disappointments are dissipated, but at the same time be careful not to set up conditioning that may carry disastrous results for the future. There is life after the next ten minutes.

When the time comes for children to make important choices that will seriously affect their lives, parents hope their children will act wisely. Hoping is not enough. *Consciously* developing a plan to help children accumulate principles and skills to successfully discriminate between the negative and positive influences is important because influences are present almost everywhere. Discriminating skills, of course, are not suddenly bestowed upon children at fourteen or twenty-one by their fairy godmother. It takes time and practice to acquire the necessary tools, so discriminating practice should be started early.

Start by verbalizing your own discriminating intentions, skills, and principles as early as the children can begin to grasp what you mean. Just to be discriminating yourself is not enough for you as a parent. Children learn some things just by watching their parents' example (for better or for worse), but we found that talking about making choices with the children *during receptive moments* and as succinctly as possible is usually necessary to get them to focus their attention on the idea and the principle. Keep the principles active in the family consciousness. Too tired to bother? Invest consciously for a period of time, and then, after awhile, the children will begin to be discriminating with little or no energy required on your part. You'll be glad you did.

Parents can help their children learn to make positive choices for their lives by giving them a pattern of judgment to follow, such as "When Uncle Matthew visits, we're going to request that he not smoke in our house," "I'm not going to watch that TV program because I don't want to take that junk into my mind," "We won't be inviting Daniel to dinner because his habit of using so much foul language is not something we want to hear in our house." These discriminating comments, that are based on carefully chosen family principles, need to be accompanied with the utmost kindness toward the person, respecting that person's right to her or his personal choices and making it clear the person is not being discriminated against, but the *behavior* is.

Help your children, by your example, develop the confidence to be able to make value judgments for their minds, bodies, and lives so that when you aren't around to guide, they can say, "Not in my mind!" "Not in my body!" "Not in my life!"

We worked together as a family on discriminating principles for the welfare of each one and for the whole family. Jill and Jim came to understand the importance of our efforts to keep negative influences out of our home and out of our lives. Because they felt valuable, appreciated, and secure, it was easier for them to recognize and keep out of the house negative influences that came to their attention. They commented on the differences they observed between our home life and the lives and homes of some of their peers; they felt honored to be a part of our family project.

There is a choice! A place of pandemonium has a shaky foundation of confusion, tension, and dissatisfaction, flimsy walls of uncertainty and insecurity, and a leaky roof of emotional fragmentation. In contrast, a home that is a sanctuary has a foundation of principles and positive mechanisms for solving problems. A sanctuary has sturdy walls of wisdom and love, and a solid roof of joy.

Creating for your family a sanctuary to call home is so worthwhile! This atmosphere is a special gift of joy for the entire family. The bonus for your children is that as you create the family sanctuary atmosphere, you help them develop the ability to be discriminating, so someday they, too, will confidently declare, "Not in our house!"

29.

THE HOLIDAYS ARE COMING!

Y es, THE HOLIDAYS ARE COMING; we can't wait! We're overjoyed to contemplate them, right? Well, not exactly. People with families generally think, with some trepidation, about all the work of preparations and the whole different set of dynamics that surrounds the holiday season. They hope the good times will balance out the stress. People without families sometimes dread the holidays for different reasons; for example, they anticipate feeling lonely.

Is it possible to anticipate the holidays with joy and appreciation without the dread of stress? We think so, but careful thought and planning are needed because our culture seems to shift into frantic gear at holiday time.

Holiday panic doesn't have to happen in your house. Determine that this year will be different, and start the shift by making a list of what will make the difference, for instance, experiencing no stress. Usually the Mom's experience determines whether a family's holidays are delightful or dreadful. If you, the Mom, are genuinely enjoying yourself, the family will. If you are having a dreadful time, probably everyone else in the family will as well. Both enjoyment and misery can be contagious; preplanning can avoid misery and provide enjoyment. Start by working out a plan to escape the trap of the Supermom/Wonderwoman role. Only Mom can keep herself from slipping into that role because everyone else seems to make the assumption that Mom can and will do-it-all. In order to avoid getting tricked, carefully examine what doing-it-all generally means. Perhaps Mom's role includes far more than is really necessary to provide a successful and joyous holiday time.

As the holidays approach and we get caught up in the holiday spirit, spending more than is wise for presents, meals, decorations, and entertainment sometimes just seems to happen. Foolish spending creates stress on the parents which adversely affects the entire family. By *consciously* choosing and following spending limits, you can have family fun without limits because lavish spending is not a requirement for enjoyable holidays.

Your plans for the holiday season may include extended family, and perhaps friends as well. Children often feel left out and ignored as the adults become involved with one another. Special consideration for the children, including the babies, can prevent them from being overlooked in the crowd. Using the principle of balance wisely can assure that each member of your immediate family—Mom, Dad, and each child—feels good about the holidays without unduly neglecting your guests. Sometimes departing from the usual holiday format is refreshing. If you would like to try some new ideas, you may find that in sharing the ideas with members of the extended family, they would like some changes as well, but haven't had the courage to suggest them.

What would the holidays be without traditions! They usually play a major role in most holiday celebrations. As you are considering the various facets of your celebrations, scrutinize the traditions from both your and your spouse's childhood families. Just because your moms and grandmothers carried on a particular tradition, doesn't mean you and your family must. Include the family in choosing *your* family's traditions. Re-examine the traditions each year. Particular ones don't have to be practiced every year; some very nice holiday events may be right only once. Determine to be flexible and not become a slave to traditions. Traditions can be the source of burdens and disappointments, but handled wisely, they can enrich the pleasure and joy of the holidays.

An unexpected holiday surprise can be a lot of fun. A decorating surprise was especially enjoyed during one Christmas day in our house. We made a gingerbread house for each person and furnished frosting and candies for decorating. The various creations were fabulous, and we had a whimsical gingerbread village for the rest of the day. Then the houses gradually disappeared as our guests went home, but the happy memories of the event remained.

Fast forward to January 2, and think about what each member of your family would consider to be happy memories of the holidays, and use those ideas in your plans. And of course, invite further suggestions. One year we had macaroni and cheese for Christmas dinner. That was the kids' choice, and they were proud and delighted as we sat down to eat. Inviting them to make that decision and joyfully honoring it, added so much fun to the occasion.

Have the courage to do a Holiday Overhaul for your family. Choose not to drift along with the cultural frenzy, but instead, to create a special, relaxed holiday that each member of the family remembers as, "Now *that* was the year!"

30.

WHAT ABOUT SANTA CLAUS?

TELLING SMALL CHILDREN the story of Santa Claus as if it were gospel truth, and then continuing the fantasy for years as the children grow is traditional in our culture. Often parents do this without thinking, just because Santa Claus is a traditional part of Christmas, their parents practiced the tradition with them when they were children, and many other parents are also practicing the tradition. Since so many people are telling their children the story of Santa Claus, how could there be anything wrong?

Many adults have shared with us that they felt betrayed by their parents when they found out the Santa Claus story was a hoax. They remember asking Santa in complete faith for certain gifts, and then trying really hard to be good, but the gifts weren't under the Christmas tree. "What happened? Wasn't I good enough? Doesn't Santa like me? Tommy and Sue got what *they* wanted." Adult memories of Christmas morning disappointments and personal questioning was the theme of a movie a few years ago, and recently an anchor man on television related, "It was a major trauma for me to learn that the Santa Claus in the store was just a helper."

This feeling of betrayal is not uncommon. Many adults have memories of the pain of learning they had been led to believe something that wasn't true. These are wounds that have lasted into adulthood and in subtle ways affected life for them. Is there a way for your family to enjoy all the Christmas traditions without your children experiencing this kind of disappointment?

There is definitely a risk in *seriously* telling children the story of Santa Claus coming from the North Pole in a sleigh with lots of toys in his pack, landing on their roof, coming down their chimney, and leaving gifts only if they are good, because this is a deception. Seriously guiding the children to put out cookies and milk, and then taking them away after the children have gone to sleep is also a deception. Yet these same parents would be angry and distressed if their children lied to and deceived *them*.

The issue here is the serious deception of children who have matured enough to have definite expectations of Santa and his marvelous pack of gifts. To children who are quite small, stories of Santa Claus and his reindeer fit in right along side other fanciful stories such as *The Cat in the Hat*. Somehow little children know it's a game. All these stories fit into their imaginative world as play—fun to hear and daydream about. The little ones play with their toys and don't think about getting more on some future day called Christmas. This is a joyful time, and as the children grow, it seems wise for parents to help them peacefully move to another stage of understanding without engaging in deception and risking their disappointment, and perhaps, trauma.

One approach for the next stage of understanding would be to present Santa as representing the spirit of Christmas giving—the spirit of Santa Claus. While the concept of Santa can drift into the wonderful world of imagination along with elves, unicorns, and *The Cat in the Hat,* the *spirit* of Santa can become the spirit behind a playful *let's pretend* game. In this Santa Claus game the emphasis on Santa Claus shifts from getting to *giving*.

When your children are mature enough to understand and enjoy pretending, they are ready, with a little help from Mommy or Daddy, to pretend to be Santa Claus by giving a gift from Santa Claus to someone else. The fun of secretly knowing that they are the Santa that gave the surprise gift will delight them. In turn, when *they* receive a gift from Santa Claus, they can also delight in knowing that someone else is playing the game of pretending to be Santa Claus for them.

The Santa Claus game ends with delightful memories; in contrast, the traditional Santa Claus fantasy often ends with disappointment and disillusionment. In fact, the Santa Claus *game* doesn't have to end. It can go on for many years, even into adulthood, with the same childlike delight each time the pretend Santa gives in secret. The secret may only last a few moments, but the happy memories of family fun with this Santa Claus game can last a lifetime.

The story of Santa Claus with his bottomless pack perpetuates the expectation of infinite *getting* of whatever one puts on the list for Santa and encourages self-centeredness. Even making the list is risky business, because a child could be devastated if everything on it isn't under the tree on Christmas morning. The naughty or nice aspect of Santa's supposed giving can set up needless fears and anxieties in children who take Santa seriously. This whole scenario puts parents in a very awkward position. Could it be that the true spirit of Santa Claus is to give unconditionally just because you are *you*?

The Santa Claus game relieves the possibility of financial stress, because parents need not get caught up in trying to fulfill the fantasy of the Santa Claus story. Parents attempting to make the fantasy come true cannot explain that Santa Claus can't afford the toys the children want; therefore, they often become susceptible to the marketing ploys of toy companies, spending far more than is wise at Christmas time. The budget is strained, sometimes for months, and family stress results. Children unknowingly feel the stress, and therefore, are burdened as well. Children are very sensitive to the undercurrents in their home. An important principle of parenting is to choose long-term value (no stress) over short-term comfort (unwisely giving the latest fad gifts just because the children have been hypnotized into believing there are particular toys they *must have*). Giving the children a household free of stress can be the best Christmas gift of all.

By adopting for your family a non-traditional approach to Santa Claus, you have an opportunity to demonstrate to your children that your family does special things, and, at the same time, they are also learning important principles. This is also an opportunity for your children to learn to keep certain traditions and family practices special within the family, and to honor the fact that other families' traditions may be different and the privacy of other families should also be respected.

We suggest that, as your children become ready, you gracefully transform the cultural Santa Claus into a deception-free Santa Claus game. The children will love to play the game because they'll feel important and valuable. Mom and Dad can also enjoy Santa without the usual stress of pulling off the traditional Santa Claus thing. In your family Santa will be transformed into an enduring symbol of the joy of *unconditional giving.*

31.

HELP!

Bill: Jennifer called one afternoon to share with us the news that her teenage son, Paul, had made a very unwise decision and the results were disastrous for him and the family. She knew it would be difficult, but not impossible, to straighten out the situation; however, her greatest sorrow was that he had not asked her or his Dad for advice. She wailed, "Why, oh, why didn't he come to us?"

DURING THE CONVERSATION I asked Jennifer, "When you were a teenager and a young adult, did you consult with your parents or other wise adults with more experience and insight who could give you a better perspective?"

"Oh no, of course not," she blurted in a spontaneous rush. "I was always quite capable of thinking for myself—after all, I had become an adult, so I didn't need to ask anyone for advice. Besides that, if I ever was in doubt or needed confirmation, I just checked with my girlfriends." Then she stopped. Dead silence hung on the phone for a few seconds, then she laughed softly and said, "Boy, I walked into that one, didn't I?"

I explained that there is a program in our culture that leads people to believe that if they have reached eighteen they are an adult, and therefore, they are *supposed* to know everything without asking.

Paul is eighteen now and has absorbed that program. Perhaps without even consciously realizing it, Paul didn't ask for help because he was fearful he would lose his grown-up identity. That fear keeps many young people from benefiting by helpful new information and advice.

Jennifer realized that her son had been caught in this erroneous belief, as she, herself, had been when she was younger. I assured her that nearly everyone is affected by this cultural program, so it certainly isn't personal to her or to her son. I explained further that those who are caught in this cultural program don't realize they've simply picked up the script and are playing it out, believing they are thinking for themselves. The way one becomes free is to realize that a *really* secure teenager or adult, one who is independent of the cultural beliefs, can accept that to ask for help is mature. *Not* to ask for help when one has never gone through a particular experience and has no personal past knowledge and experience to draw upon is immature. Being free of the cultural program requires redefining, according to what's *true,* what it means to be an adult.

A mature adult is one who realizes that it's o.k. not to know everything, but rather to realize that "I don't know" at each stage of life. Sometimes we can't even ask questions because we don't know what the questions are. We *all* can benefit greatly from the wisdom of those who have gone through any particular stage before us—as a teenager, as a college student, or as a young single person establishing a career; whether dating, courting, beginning married life, parenting, or establishing a business or relationship. Making the best choice is difficult without experience and wisdom, so it is good common sense to try to avoid making mistakes. I suggested that Jennifer begin sharing with her children in a casual, off-hand, and indirect way how she has found value in having a mentor.

I also suggested that she find ways that would be most meaningful to her particular children to help them grasp such truths as:

✧ *It is mature and o.k. to realize you don't have all the answers and to consult others whom you know to be experienced and wise.* This attitude is really what being adult is about. The grown-up person who declares, "I have all the answers, even though I've never gone through this before," is not really an adult.

Help!

❖ *It's an adult approach to seek wisdom in order to save oneself from learning the hard way.* The trouble with taking the risk to learn the hard way is that sometimes that kind of learning leads down a lifelong path you didn't want to be on, but that you can get stuck on. Sometimes learning the hard way can lead you *and those with you* right over the cliff and there is no return at all. Your friends or your spouse or children don't deserve that.

❖ *It should be, and really is, o.k. to have a mentor.* Having a business mentor is common, and no one feels less of an adult because they have one. How about a mentor for life in general? How about a mentor for a day? The possibilities are limitless.

❖ *Stumbling around in the dark is childish.* People don't usually realize they are in the dark, just like fish don't realize they're in water, or humans don't think about the fact they are moving about in air. One of the first steps toward getting out of the dark is to know you are in the dark. The second step is to find someone who can help you find a light switch.

❖ *It's o.k. to ask one's mentor, "Do you see anything I'm not seeing, that if I changed, my life would be better?"* This is maturely observing, "I don't know what questions to ask."

❖ *Peers don't usually make good mentors.* Peers can be wonderful friends, and they may have gone through a particular experience that can help you. If your buddy has fixed his car, and you've never worked on a car, ask him for ideas so you can fix your own car, but not about planning your financial future, understanding women, or starting your career. A good mentor has a much broader perspective of life than one can normally find with peers.

❖ *Not everyone who has gone through an experience or a particular stage in life before you is automatically a good mentor.* Look for wisdom, enlightenment, principles, new ideas, and objectivity, and find someone who is free of the cultural program. Don't overlook parents as mentors; that's a possibility often missed. You have an edge if you find someone who cares about you.

✧ *The benefits of having a mentor are a smoother, happier, and more efficient life.*

Jennifer appreciated the mentoring immensely and sighed, "Oh, I wish I'd known about this earlier. Giving my son this information long ago may have avoided the fix we're in now." I encouraged her not to bemoan the past, but to get busy and devise the most diplomatic way she can find to lead her children to see what it really means to be an adult. One sure sign of maturity is having mentors.

32.

THE CHEERFUL CHILD

Living with *cheerful* children is a joy. Life is more fun, nourishing, and productive in a cheerful atmosphere. When children are cheerful, they are:
• *in a good place with themselves and others,*
• *free of many of the common fears,*
• *more likely to be in good health, and*
• *freer to be creative and to fulfill their potential.*

WHAT MAKES A CHILD CHEERFUL? Is it being in pleasant physical surroundings, being in good health, or being with cheerful adults? All of these factors are certainly positive, but there are many children with these advantages who are not cheerful. This is the answer! What truly makes a child cheerful is a fundamental positive attitude based on knowing about her or his true invisible Self and Self-value, and having the ability to live in accordance with that value. Small children don't need to know and recognize true Self and Self-value consciously. They do need to have adults around them who know it for them, so they can intuitively sense these intrinsic qualities. Cheerfulness comes naturally when the vital ingredients are in place.

The deepest longing of every individual is to *know* that she or he is valuable. Self-confidence comes from having an internalized set of values that enables an individual to make the right choices for daily living. *The cheerful child feels intrinsically valuable and confident.*

COMPARING AND COMPETING

In one of our study group meetings, Carolyn asked, "How can I help my children feel valuable? I thought I was working on this, but they aren't cheerful."

> *Bill: You need to help your children take three steps: appreciate their true Self, recognize their intrinsic value, and then develop, by their own process, a value system based on those elements.*

"But it's hard to know what to do," said Carolyn.

> *Bill: Yes, it is. First of all, it's important to know what not to do. Don't follow the culture. It will lead you to external world value judgments instead of leading you to your children themselves, where the answer really is. Following our culture usually sets up children to be vulnerable to feelings of failure because there is a flip side to every success. The side you land on determines how you feel. For instance, Molly may play perfectly in a piano recital one week and feel great. The next week a term paper that she poured much time and energy into garners a C grade, and she plunges into depression. The following week is her birthday and her parents give her a car. Wow! The kids really think she's terrific now. In a couple more weeks the boy she'd been hoping would ask her for a date, doesn't, and she begins to see an ugly, worthless image in the mirror. And so she goes week after week, month after month, riding the self-worth roller coaster that constantly goes up and down.*

The comparison/competition arena is the culprit. All comparisons and all competition are oriented "out there." Do I have more friends than Susie has? How pretty am I? How well do I perform in soccer? Will I win the spelling bee? Did I read more books than Melody? Did I play better than anyone else at the recital? I won! I lost!

The Cheerful Child

Parents encourage their children to excel in everything. But how can all of the children win in competition? What happens to the emotional core of the ones who don't win? What happens to those who do win when the next game is different? The sense of worth of those who lose plunges to "Oh, I'm worthless." Many parents have told us Johnny or Judy absolutely must be in competitive sports in order to feel good about themselves. The truth is, Johnny or Judy must feel very good about themselves *before* going into the sport in order to escape emotional trauma if they lose or make a mistake. They even need to feel good about themselves to handle winning well. Children must feel valuable first or competitive activities are much more potentially damaging than they are potentially beneficial.

The principle here might be stated:
A child needs to already feel valuable in order to withstand the pressure and the vicissitudes of the comparison/competition/achievement arena.

WHAT CAN I DO?

O.K. So the comparison/competitive arena is to be avoided, but you ask, "What *positive* actions can I take to help my child feel valuable?" The most positive actions you can take are the ones that communicate to your child, first, *your own* valuing of your true Self, and, second, your valuing of *herSelf* or *himSelf*. Valuing a child is very different from protective love or possessive love. It is honoring the feelings, the thoughts, and the magic of the child.

Next, counteract the message that tells children that clumsiness at a skill or getting a grade lower than an A is a deficit in their personal value. One way to avoid this pitfall is to constantly praise success in *trying*. Little Ryan loves to play golf with a wooden spoon and a nerf ball. We are careful to respond to his less-than-perfectly executed efforts with the same smile and lilt in our voices as when he perfectly executes a swing: "That was a wonderful try, Sweetie!"

Ryan is free of the fear of failure when he knows that genuinely *trying* is just as o.k. as succeeding according to the usual cultural standards. This freedom allows him to feel valuable *just as he is,* not for what he accomplishes. This is an important shift in thinking.

WHAT ABOUT SELF-VALUE?

The cultural program to feel valuable emphasizes *external* focus, and motivation generally becomes a seeking for something out there that is often beyond one's reach or control. The search usually begins with trying to please parents, then later peers, teachers, employers, spouses, one's children, and so on throughout life. This quest becomes an obsession to be liked and to win approval from others. But the quest is rarely satisfied because the first requirement hasn't been put into place: liking oneself. The secret of liking oneself is discovering Self-value.

> • Self-value is a confident recognition that who I truly am is not captured in the image in the mirror, but is invisible, wonderful, and *infinitely* valuable.
> • Self-value is inherent and fixed, not good one day and bad another.
> • Self-value is not dependent upon what I can accomplish, how well I do things, what I have, or what others think of me.
> • No one can take my Self-value from me.
> • Self-value is something that is true about you as a parent and true about your children.

A true sense of Self-value isn't fragile. There is a solid feeling of satisfaction and well-being generated by self-approval: "I am o.k. because of my inherent value. Yes, I make mistakes sometimes, but that does not mean I am not valuable." The emotional core is free of fear after a child discovers and operates from Self-value; therefore, the child is cheerful and can act with confidence and joy.

THE VALUE SYSTEM

Now here is a parenting gem:
A value system that your children develop that is based on the truth of their own Self-value is not vulnerable to peer pressure, fads of the moment, or other external influences.

Your child builds the structure of a durable value system as she or he adopts useful principles and guidelines that support the truth of her or his own Self-value. Children cannot do this alone. When the principle of Self-value is unknown to parents, they can only attempt to transfer their own value systems onto their children as one would give a child a jacket and tell her or him to wear it. A jacket can easily be taken off and discarded, and so, too, transferred values can easily be abandoned. But when parents know the principle of Self-value and recognize and honor their child's true Self, the parents can then help their child build a positive value system on her or his recognition of Self-value. *These values* are not easily abandoned because they are directly related to the child's own sense of Self-value. When an individual knows and enjoys a sense of personal guidance and support that works in freedom, how could that person, adult or child, be other than cheerful?

A positive guide and strong support throughout life for your child includes:

- your child's sense of true Self,
- your child's own recognition of Self-value, and
- your child's developing and using a value system based on that recognition.

These three elements combine synergistically to provide a powerful resource for joyful living.

THE FOG

If Self-value is an inherent attribute for everyone, why then, isn't everyone cheerful? The answer to this question lies in *awareness*. A marvelous benefactor could establish a million dollar bank account for you, but if you never knew it existed, it wouldn't do you any good. Furthermore, while you had this bank account, of which you were unaware, if you were told repeatedly that you were poor, you would believe something completely untrue about yourself, and that belief would be reflected in your attitudes and life. What does all this have to do with feeling valuable?

Here is the essence of feeling valuable: *Everyone's true invisible Self is marvelous, and it follows that the marvelous nature of the Self is infinitely valuable.* However, the lack of awareness of this wonder is like a thick fog that temporarily obscures the Self and Self-value. It's as if the true Self and its Self-value do not exist, and then one's attitudes and life reflect that void.

How can this lack of awareness happen? The thick fog is comprised of false beliefs from the culture, erroneous ideas acquired through direct influence, and also the effects of disturbing life experiences. Often we are tricked into believing concepts that are not true.

> **Win:** *Recently my mother told me that when she was a child and young adult, it seemed that everyone around her—relatives, teachers, parents of her friends, her Sunday School teacher, and even her own parents—informed her in subtle and not so subtle ways: "You have many short-comings." "You'll never do things well." "You're not too intelligent." Even though she now knows intellectually that those judgments were not correct, she is still burdened emotionally by this early programming. Just think how different her whole life would have been had the people in her younger life recognized her true Self and Self-value, helping her to recognize them herself and to live accordingly! Often a person does not recognize and accept Self-value until another recognizes and honors that truth. This is an important role parents play in their children's lives.*

VALUE-BASED RELATIONSHIPS

The two of us approached the whole area of personal value by, first, acknowledging that there is great value in ourSelf, and, second, acknowledging that same quality in each other. When this mutual understanding was in place solidly for us, it was easy to drop the temptations to condemn ourselves or to criticize each other. Of course, we weren't always content with our own actions or in agreement with the other's actions, but we knew we each were doing our best at the moment and no criticism was warranted. This mode of interaction between us naturally led us also to refrain from *personally* condemning or criticizing our children, but, as parents, just to help them correct their actions and misconceptions, when necessary.

> *There is no greater gift that parents can give their children than the recognition of their children's true Self and Self-value.*

The Cheerful Child

"Your real Self, the essence of who you are, is perfect, wonderful, and valuable." We began saying this, verbally and silently, to Jill and Jim and later to our grandchildren, Deanna and Ryan, long before they could talk, and we repeated it frequently throughout their childhood. Our words were, in fact, merely reinforcing what they *already* knew without their consciously knowing they knew it, so it seemed natural to them to value themselves highly. With this as their foundation it was easy for them to be naturally cheerful in their interactions with us and with their friends.

In addition to actually talking with Jill and Jim about their value, we *recognized* their Self-value by the manner in which we talked with them about other matters in their lives. We showed them that we valued their innate ability to think and make good judgments and to act creatively and individually, and they grew to value these abilities for themselves.

Jill and Jim attended a middle class California high school when drugs were the exciting new thing and before the anti-drug programs had begun in earnest. We knew it would do no good to order them to leave drugs alone, but we talked, instead, about honoring the Self in all aspects of our lives. We related to them that we each placed immense value on our Self, and had, for instance, long ago decided not to drink or smoke because we each wanted to keep our mind clear and our body free for our Self to shine through. Then the choice had to be up to them; they were independent thinkers and formed their own value judgments concerning drugs.

Win: *One day when the drugs subject arose, Jim said to me, "I'm sorry to tell you, Mom, that my decision not to use drugs had nothing to do with you and Dad. When I'm at school, I just look across the street at the kids who go over to the park to use drugs during breaks, and I know they are the losers in life. I simply refuse to be a loser." I smiled. Jim was probably right. He wasn't particularly impressed with our decision for our own lives on the subject or with any admonitions we may have given him. But there was something that we had done throughout his childhood that we believe was a significant factor in his decision.*

Unless you chain your kids to their beds or lock them up, you can't prevent drug use once they are mature enough to be away from home on a regular basis without parents. We didn't try to restrict the children, but we believe it did make a crucial difference in Jim's case that throughout his childhood we had honored and trusted his true Self. He must have picked up and assimilated the message in his consciousness. When he had to make his choice—to get into drugs, or not—his recognition of his Self-value was such that there was no way in the world he would consider himself a loser and use drugs.

TRUSTING WITHOUT FEAR

Preteens and teens benefit when their parents support and trust them to develop *by their own process* a value system that is based on their own acceptance of their Self-value. They then have a value system that is really their own and not one imposed arbitrarily upon them. If your children have traveled this path, you do not need to have fears. When a child has developed a value system by her or his own process, there is familiarity with, and confidence in, each element. Then when a child faces a challenge, she or he can quickly bring to mind the values needed to confidently walk through the experience.

"I'm going down to the cafe, Mom," Jill announced one summer evening when she was home from college. She told us later about the evening, "One of the kids told us that there was a party at Doug's house. I thought that a party at Doug's would be an o.k. party." On the way she became paired up with Ken, whom she'd seen before, but did not know.

Jill continued, "I was really surprised that not long after we got there, a [marijuana] joint was being passed around. Ken sat to my left and the joint was coming around from the right. When it got to me, I just passed it on to Ken without smoking it, then he passed it on without smoking it. We were the only ones who just passed it on. Later, when the crowd broke up, Ken said to me, 'I've been having trouble with that stuff and thought I was the only one who didn't want it. I know I wouldn't have been able to pass it on if you hadn't been there and done what you did. Thanks!'" Jill finished with, "I wasn't even thinking about Ken. I'm glad, though, that what I did helped him."

What was going on here? Long before that party, Jill had developed a sense of her Self-value and, by her own independent thinking, a value system based on that. She had told us earlier, "I've got to keep my body and my mind free of drugs so I can live like I want. Anybody who doesn't like me for that isn't friend material." So she wasn't vulnerable to the peer pressure at the party.

APPRECIATION DAYS

Joyful family living! What does it take? An ongoing activity that our entire family enjoyed was special Appreciation Days. These special days were always a surprise for an honored family member. Although we didn't talk much about it, the underlying principle of these special occasions was to show that the family appreciated the true Self and the Self-value of that person. On our Appreciation Days a long and enjoyable Treasure Hunt always led to a pile of gifts. We also planned special activities such as going to a restaurant or movie, or playing the honored one's choice of a game.

We didn't know that Jim had made elaborate plans for an evening out on one of his Appreciation Days, and he didn't tell us until after we'd revealed the surprise. "Go ahead, Jim; it's o.k. with us. We'll do it tomorrow night." But he declined the offer with a smile, "Oh no, I can't wait," and we carried on with a joyful evening.

Ideas for an Appreciation Day can be endless and varied according to each person and each family, and they are such fun. Our Appreciation Days were distinctly different from birthdays in that they were not tied to an obligation, but were enjoyed on spontaneously selected days as a complete surprise for the honored family member.

✧ ✧ ✧

Our children's cheerful attitude was a direct result of the confidence they had in their own Self-value as a person and their own value system based on that Self-value. Because their sense of value was recognized at home, they did not *need* further recognition from their peers or other outside persons. They did not *need* friends to be cheerful, but because they *were* cheerful they had many good quality friends. They did not *need* achievements to feel good about themselves, but because they valued themselves so highly, they chose viable areas in which to succeed, and achieved success.

Children are naturally cheerful, and we parents can help them remain cheerful throughout childhood, and, hopefully, throughout the rest of their lives, by honoring their true Self, their Self-value and their own development of their value system. For us, this underlying cheerfulness and the appreciation of each family member's true Self and Self-value combined to make living with our children truly joyful.

EPILOGUE

THE ADVENT OF THE NEW MILLENNIUM is making society more receptive than ever before to change. Ideas and insights that were very uncommon when we were actively parenting will be better supported for you, dear reader, than they were for us. In fact, there is already a great deal of evidence of this acceptance of change in our culture. This shift provides you with rich opportunities to pursue new, enlightened parenting guidance, such as we have shared with you in this book.

We have come to believe that the greatest gift of love we can give to our children is to live joyfully with them. We invite you to take what you wish from this book and build on it, adding your own insights and enlightenment as you experience new frontiers. Your gift of living joyfully with your children is a gift not only to your children, but as they carry these ideas on into their own families, a gift to your grandchildren, and their children as well. Your gift of love will be felt for generations.

It's all a wonderful adventure! We wish you the same enjoyment, excitement, and eager anticipation of what will be coming next as we have experienced, and still do.

As we close these pages dedicated to enlightened parenting, we want to pay tribute to our wonderful parents who gave us each a happy and loving childhood.

Evelyn and John Grau

Gladys and Charles Sweet